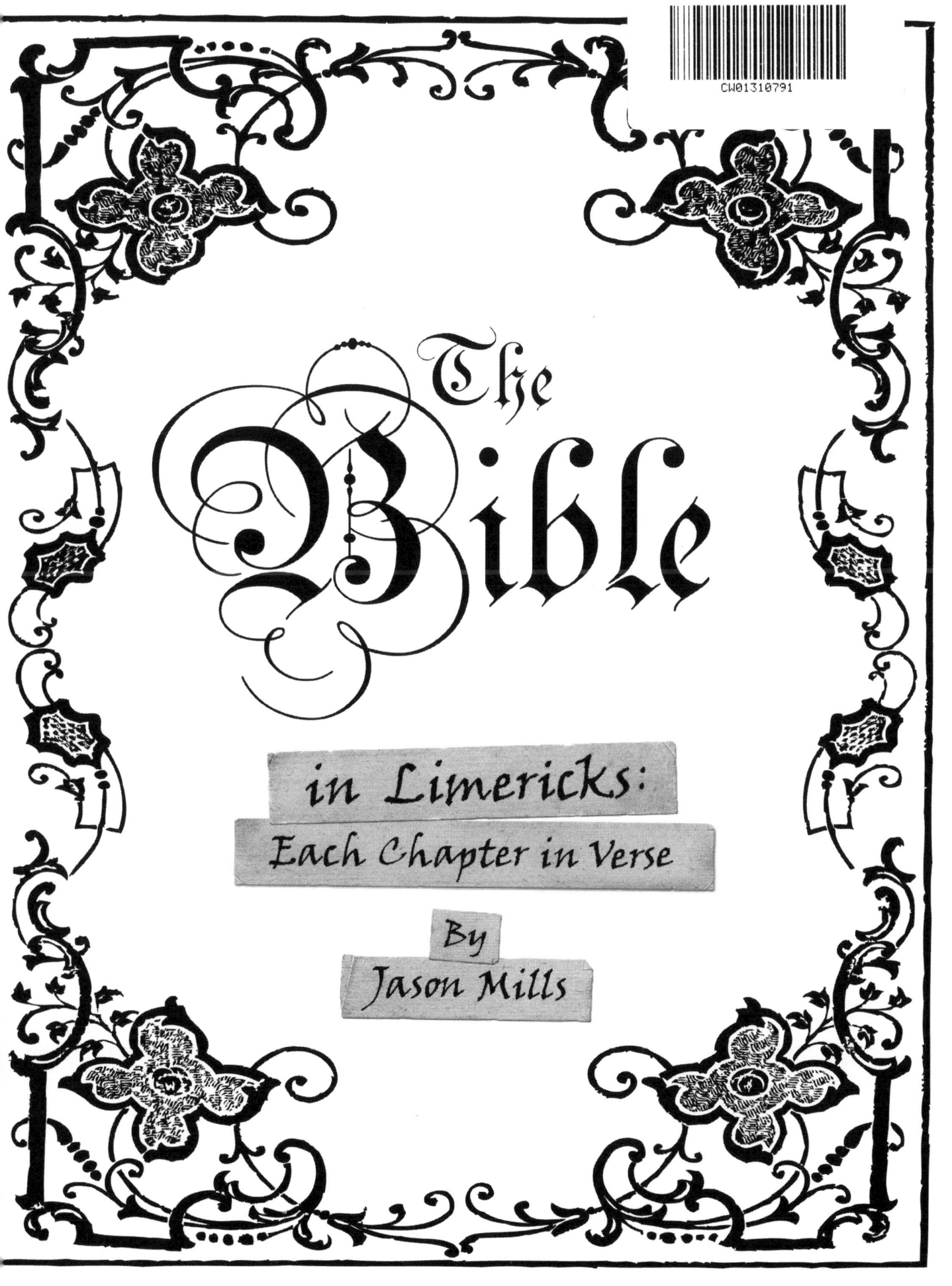

ISBN-13: 978-1530530236

Copyright © Jason Mills 2016

Cover and title page © Simon Tranter
http://www.simonleetranter.co.uk/

The right of Jason Mills to be identified as the Author of the Work has been asserted by him in accordance with the Copyrights, Designs and Patents Act 1988.

All rights reserved. No part of this publication may be reproduced, distributed or transmitted in any form or by any means (electronic, mechanical, photocopying, recording or otherwise) without the prior permission of the copyright holders.

CONTENTS

Preface..5

OLD TESTAMENT..........................7

Genesis...9
Exodus..12
Leviticus.......................................15
Numbers.......................................18
Deuteronomy................................20
Joshua..23
Judges..25
Ruth...26
1 Samuel......................................27
2 Samuel......................................29
1 Kings...31
2 Kings...33
1 Chronicles.................................34
2 Chronicles.................................37
Ezra...39
Nehemiah....................................40
Esther..41
Job...42
Psalms...45
Proverbs......................................56
Ecclesiastes.................................58
Song of Solomon.........................59
Isaiah...60
Jeremiah......................................65
Lamentations...............................69
Ezekiel...69
Daniel..73
Hosea..74
Joel..75
Amos...75
Obadiah.......................................76
Jonah...76
Micah..77

Nahum...77
Habakkuk....................................78
Zephaniah...................................78
Haggai...78
Zechariah....................................79
Malachi.......................................80

NEW TESTAMENT........................81

Matthew......................................83
Mark..85
Luke..86
John..88
Acts of the Apostles....................89
Romans.......................................91
1 Corinthians..............................93
2 Corinthians..............................94
Galatians....................................95
Ephesians...................................95
Philippians..................................96
Colossians..................................96
1 Thessalonians..........................97
2 Thessalonians..........................97
1 Timothy...................................97
2 Timothy...................................98
Titus...98
Philemon....................................99
Hebrews.....................................99
James.......................................100
1 Peter......................................100
2 Peter......................................101
1 John.......................................101
2 John.......................................101
3 John.......................................102
Jude..102
Revelation................................102

PREFACE

Apologia

Gentle reader, reflect as you eye this:
I may not be the first one to try this,
    But I hope mine's the best,
    So tell your friends, lest
You end up as the last one to buy this!

Version

I've mostly gone off the King James:
By royal appointment, its fame's
    Well deserved, for its prose is
    As splendid as Moses -
Which brings up another thing: names.

Names

Biblical names, long and alien,
Confound anyone not an Israeli, an'
    Most of us ain't,
    So I've quickened the quaint,
Lopped the long, squashed the sesquipedalian.

Rhythm

Though the scansion is generally fine,
The reader might welcome a sign
    As to where the weight falls,
    So if rhythm appals
Place the stress on the grey underline.

Concision

Some chapters fit five lines with ease;
For others the dense plot's a squeeze.
    If it doesn't make sense
    I can say in defence
The original too is a tease!

Interpretation

If my tone here is often light-hearted,
I hope I've not too far departed
    From the KJV text:
    It's not broken, just flexed.
But enough about me, let's get started!

GENESIS

1
And God declared: "Let there be light,
"Sky, land, sea, plants, sun, moon, day and night,
   "Fish, birds, beasts, then a man,
   "Woman too -" (Here the plan
Hung a left, and has never gone right.)

2
God breatheth life into dust,
Told Adam in Eden, "You must
   "Eat naught of that tree!
   "Here's a rib-girl for thee."
Lacking shame, shame they'd lacklustre lust.

3
"Go on, have some fruit," hissed the snake.
So they did, and God yelled, "For God's sake!
   "Serpent, crawl! Woman, cry!
   "Now begone from mine eye!
"And for you, Adam, work! And backache."

4
Their kids were a handful. Young Cain
Killed Abel. "Just look at that stain!"
   Cried God in his wrath.
   "Blood never comes off!
"You're marked, son. Don't do it again!"

5
They had long boring lives in those days.
Having kids when too old was the craze.
   There was nothing to see,
   And not much on TV,
But it's Noah's bit next anyways.

6
There were too many folks, and too bad.
God had goofed and was troubled and sad.
   He decreed: "Genocide!
   "Noah, get thee inside
"A big boat full of beasts!" (Was he mad?!)

7
In twos and fourteens came the wights.
Seven days passed, then forty wet nights.
   Other numbers to note:
   They were five months afloat,
With just eight proto-Israelites.

8
So at last Noah sent a bird out:
Found dry land! And so, ever devout,
   He sacrificed critters:
   "Heads up, God, here's your fritters!"
God savoured: "No more floods I'll spout!"

9
"Here's a rainbow! Now get things in shape.
"Be fruitful!" So Noah chose grape.
   Drunk and naked he snored,
   Which his youngest abhorred:
"Aww, Dad, at least throw on a cape!"

10
After the moist megadeath
Came the sons of Shem, Ham and Japheth.
   Canaan! That's the gist.
   Let's skip the full list:
We would only be wasting our breath.

11
The folks built a tower and conversed.
God was annoyed: "You're all cursed!
   "You'll babble! Unstable,
   "You rabble, is Babel!"
Confounded, confused, they dispersed.

12
To Egypt went Abram and wife.
"Say you're my sis, for my life!"
   The King took the bait,
   But God plagued him. "Now, wait!
"Have her back, there's no need for this strife!"

13
"There's not enough land for us both,"
Said Abram, "So let's take an oath:
   "You take Sodom, I'll stay."
   So Lot went away.
God said, "Ha! Now let's talk about growth..."

14
Four kings contended with five
And poor Lot was taken alive!
    Abram, now ruffled,
    Killed off the kerfuffle.
"No prize! It's enough to survive."

15
At God's word, Abram cut up his pets.
God said, "**Those that this fellow begets**
    "**Will have slavish careers**
    "**For four hundred years,**
"**But don't worry, this God pays his debts.**"

16
Said Sarai, "Go get Hagar with child."
Abram did, but the women were riled.
    Hagar fled, cried "Alack!"
    God told her: "**Go back!**"
She gave birth and 'twas all reconciled.

17
Said God: "**You are Abraham now!**
"**My covenant I re-avow.**
    "**You'll need foreskins cut off.**"
    Abe swallowed a cough:
"I suppose it's less weight anyhow!"

18
"**You'll soon be a mum!**" (Sarah giggled.)
"**I'm off to blast Sodom.**" This niggled:
    "The righteous will die,"
    Abe protested. "And why?"
"**Meh, for ten I'll forget it,**" God wriggled.

19
Men of Sodom, too friendly, went blind.
Poor Lot left his saltwife behind.
    The cities were damned.
    His lusty girls planned:
Wined and dined him, then started to grind...

20
The king took Abe's nonagenarian
Wife; but God spluttered, "**Barbarian!**
    "**She's half-sister, full wife!**
    "**If you value your life,**
"**Let her and Abe go be agrarian!**"

21
At last Sarah bore Abe a son,
Isaac, and urged Abe to shun
    Poor Hagar again,
    With Ishmael. Then
Abe and Abi had beef, lamb and fun.

22
"**Go kill Isaac,**" God told Abe one day.
Nothing loath, Abe was soon on his way.
    "**I was joking!**" cried God.
    "**You're a biddable sod.**
"**But cook me this ram, *consommé*.**"

24
At one-twenty-seven died Sarah:
A good innings, one cannot say fairer.
    After her death,
    Ephron of Heth
Gave a cave grave to Abe to inter 'er.

25
"No Canaanite wife for my boy!"
Abe declared. Said his worthy envoy:
    "I'll find me a dame 'ere
    In Mesopotamia."
Thus Rebekah joined Camel Convoy.

26
Abe died and Isaac had twins
By Rebekah. Then trouble begins:
    Hunter Esau was hairy
    But sadly unwary:
Sold his birthright for Jacob's din-dins.

26
In the Philistine lands, Isaac tells
That his wife is his sis. (Parallels?)
    King Abi is cross:
    "You'll upset the Big Boss!"
Isaac wanders around digging wells.

27
"Esau, go bring me a steak!"
Said blind Isaac. Rebekah grabbed Jake.
    She gave him cooked goat
    And the goat's hairy coat,
So Dad's blessing then fell on the fake.

28

Said Isaac, "Jake, look for a mate!"
Jake wandered, and when it got late
    He used stones for his bed,
    Dreamed a ladder and said,
"My pillow's a pillar! God's great!"

29

Sheepish Rachel was wooed by Jake's water.
Jake told Laban, "I'll marry your daughter."
    'Twas dark, couldn't see 'er!
    Spent all night with Leah!
Grumbled at Pa, "Why I oughtta–!"

30

Rachel's maid was her surrogate mum.
Sister Leah would not be outdone.
    What with wives, kids and cattle
    And various chattel,
Jacob said, "See how rich I've become!"

31

Laban got grumpy, and so,
"Sod it," said Jacob, "let's go."
    Rachel nicked her dad's gods,
    Left the menfolk at odds.
"If we're bad," they agreed, "God will know."

32

Picturing Esau, Jake's pale;
He sends gifts of beasts up the trail.
    He shows off his might
    Wrestling God(?) through the night
And the stranger renames him: Israel.

33

So Jacob met Esau at last.
(It seems like their enmity's past.)
    Then Esau went back
    (Hardly worth it to pack!),
Jake to Canaan with all he'd amassed.

34

Jake's Dinah by Shechem was prized.
Said Jake's lads, "You're not circumcised!
    "You lot, slice the prepuce!"
    But they shattered the truce:
Shechem's cut kin were killed – much surprised!

35

Jacob wandered and built pillars stony.
Rachel croaked giving birth to Benoni.
    Twelve sons to his name,
    To Hebron Jake came;
Buried Isaac, then old, blind and bony.

36

This chapter lists those who are pendant
To Esau; in short, his descendants.
    There's something 'bout Zibeon
    And the smiting of Midian,
But nothing compels one's attendance.

37

"Joseph's too flashy a dresser!"
Cried his brothers. "He reckons we're lesser
    "Than he, with his dreams."
    So they went to extremes:
Potiphar became his new possessor.

38

Judah's sons Onan and Er
Gave Tamar no kids. "I'll defer
    "My third son," thought Jude;
    A decision he rued:
The harlot he slept with was her!

39

Poti's lady on Joseph would dote.
Poor Joseph behaved as he ought:
    He ran, left his clothing,
    Earned Potiphar's loathing.
(Hap she fancied not him, but his coat!)

40

Pharaoh's butler and baker said, "Joe,
"Can you understand what's apropos
    "In our symbolic dreams?"
    Joseph picked out the themes:
"You're dead, Bread; at least now you know!"

41

Of cows Pharaoh dreamed, two times seven.
Joseph said, "It's a warning from heaven!
    "At first, cornucopia,
    "Then famished dystopia.
"With prudence your appetites leaven!"

42

So to Egypt went Joe's brothers ten
To buy corn. (But they left at home Ben.)
    Joe was strange to their eyes:
    Though he called them all spies,
He sent cash, corn and kin home again.

43

Jacob's family grew hungry once more.
"Let us go and take Ben, we implore!"
    So Jacob agreed.
    Joseph answered their need
With a banquet – well, what are friends for?

44

Sneaky Joe hid a cup in Ben's sack:
"You're nicked, Ben! You nicked my knick-knack!"
    Cried Joe. "You're my slave!"
    But Judah was brave:
"Think of Jacob! Let me take the flak."

45

At that, Joseph cracked a big grin.
"You daft brothers should recognise kin!
    "It's me, whom you sold.
    "Have some land, food and gold.
"Now fetch Dad to enjoy the love-in!"

46

So Jacob, old goat, brought the kids,
Three-score plus, to peruse pyramids.
    With Rachel's and Bilhah's
    And Leah's and Zilpah's,
No wonder they'd all hit the skids!

47

Pharaoh sent Jake's lot to Goshen.
Shepherd Joe had a fortunate notion:
    "By sternest subscriptions
    "I'll fleece the Egyptians
"And put paid to this famine commotion!"

48

Joe and sons went to see dying Jake,
Jake blessed Ephraim; said: "No mistake:
    "Although he's so yout'ful,
    "Ephraim's more fruitful
"Than Manasseh. Don't bellyache!"

49

Says Jacob: "Rube, Sim and Lev fail.
"Jude's strong and Gad fights; Zeb will sail.
    "Naph's deer and Iss drudges,
    "Ben's wolfish, Dan judges,
"Ash cooks, but it's Joe who'll prevail."

50

They buried old Jake in Abe's cave.
Joe's bros (whom we know misbehave)
    Said, "Forgive us, we're fools!"
    Joe shrugged: "Meh, it's cool."
Then he followed his dad to the grave.

EXODUS

1

Joe's kith and kin died away,
But the Israelites bred and made hay.
    Pharaoh put them to work,
    Said: "These shepherdfolk irk!
"Drown their boys, it's the only safe way."

2

By the river the Pharaoh's lass found
Baby Moses, afloat and not drowned.
    But he left someone dead
    And to Midian fled;
Got wife and son too - some rebound!

3

"A bush burning!" said Moses. "That's funny…"
"It's Me! Peekaboo! Milk and honey,"
    Cried God, "for your folks
    "When they throw off their yokes."
"What's in it for me?" "Egypt's money!"

4

"Here's a cool serpent-baton. Now go.
"I'll harden the heart of Pharaoh
    "And then kill his son."
    At an inn, just for fun,
God even tried killing old Mo!

5

"Let us go have a picnic," said Moses.
Pharaoh cursed: "Every Israelite dozes!
    "Let each now make brick
    "Without straw, just as quick!"
It's all going wrong, Mo supposes!

6

"You'll be leaving soon after Passover,
"And living in Canaan in clover.
    "Now go tell your kin,"
    God went on with a grin.
"And by the way, call me Jehovah."

7

"Pharaoh's heart," said God, "I'm gonna harden.
"I don't want him begging for pardon,
    "For with plagues I will show
    "Who's the boss. This blood flow
"For starters will ruin his garden!"

8

God sent Egypt some frogs, lice and flies.
"Now release us," said Moses. "Be wise!"
    But Pharaoh was naughty,
    Hard-hearted and haughty.
(Middle East doesn't 'do' compromise...)

9

Next up, God killed all the cattle,
Then gave everyone boils. Then the rattle
    Of hail filled the land.
    "Oh, I'll meet your demand,"
Grumbled Pharaoh – but kept up the battle.

10

"I'll send locusts!" warned Mo; and he did.
Then darkness, when everyone hid.
    "All right, go, for Thoth's sake!
    "But leave your beefsteak."
Mo refused, and then Pharaoh backslid.

11

Moses rolled up his sleeves. "Right then, chum.
"It's your last chance, God's ultimatum.
    "I hereby forewarn
    "He'll kill your firstborn."
God made Pharaoh snarl: "Let it come!"

12

"Mark your door with lamb's blood, and for seven
"Days make your bread without leaven."
    Then God slew as foretold.
    "Take their silver and gold!
"Hence remember the power of Heaven!"

13

"At Passover, eat unleavened bread:
"Not leavened; unleavened instead."
    "Enough, Moses! Oy vey!
    "Let us be on our way!"
Cried his people. "Hey, why's the sea red?"

14

Moses' wind blew the Red Sea away.
(What on earth had he eaten that day?)
    Egypt followed the flight
    Of the Israelite,
But washed up on the dock of the bay.

15

Mo's people had struggled so long,
They spontaneously burst into song:
    "The Egyptians are drowned!
    "He's the best god around!"
"So obey!" said God. What could go wrong?

16

Soon they grumbled: "We're hungry and lost!"
God's eyes rolled: "Well then, let them eat frost."
    They gathered up manna
    Across the savannah:
"A bit boring," they sulked, "but low cost."

17

"We thirst!" Mo broke stone with his staff.
Josh fought Amalek plus his riff-raff.
    They went to the grave
    With Mo's Mexican wave:
No memorial, no epitaph.

18

A visit from Pops! Jethro says:
"God is great, Mo! But don't spend your days
    "On this judging malarkey:
    "Set up a hierarchy:
"You just delegate, manage, appraise!"

19

"I will manifest here in thine eye,"
Promised God, "on the top of Sinai!
    "Now go have a shower
    "And warn of my power:
"I'll obliterate whoe'er I spy nigh!"

20

"No other gods, idols, name-taking,
"Adultery, theft, sabbath-breaking;
    "Don't covet, lie, kill;
    "Keep your parents' goodwill.
"Shallow rubble for all altar-making."

21

Next come odd regulations for slavery
And stonings for some kinds of knavery.
    There's eye-for-an-eye
    And this-ox-must-die.
Lawbreakers back then showed some bravery!

22

"Here are laws about ox, sheep and corn.
"If betrothed, let no man be forsworn.
    "Make a witch be deceased,
    "And whoe'er tups a beast!
"Oh yes, and I want your firstborn."

23

"No word of a lie shalt thou breathe.
"In its ma's milk no kid shalt thou seethe.
    "As you sow and you reap,
    "So my festivals keep,
"And thine enemies' lands I bequeath."

24

Mo bled oxen. God called to the heights
Mo and six-dozen Israelites.
    They admired the glow
    Of his blue patio.
God and Mo then shared forty cold nights.

25

God rubbed his hands with a cackle:
"Now then, make me a fine tabernacle!
    "I want table and chair,
    "And a cabinet — there!
"All of gold — I want nothing ramshackle!"

26

God proceeds with his flatpack instruction
For his travelling temple construction.
    Blue, scarlet and gold,
    Watch those curtains unfold!
An impressive (if baffling) production.

27

"Make an altar for slaughtering critters,
"With lots of worked brass so it glitters.
    "There'll be pillared supports
    "For the hangings and courts.
"Aaron's line shall be always lamp-fitters."

28

"Now, costumes. For Aaron, the works:
"Robe, gems, mitre and girdle — all perks!
    "Assemble his ephod
    "By this singular method.
"And some nice uniforms for the clerks."

29

Burn, wave, sin! Drink and heave! Sweet and savoury!
Not a good time, but offerings flavour.
    God wants: bullocks and rams;
    Daily two juicy lambs;
Aaron's sons bound to ushering slavery.

30

"Keep my altar incensed, so I won't be!
"I want sweet smells when I come to haunt thee.
    "Each rubberneck'll
    "Cough up half a shekel.
"Who copies my ointment, avaunt he!"

Exodus

31
"There's this guy," God went on, "who's a tiler.
"He does metalwork too – quite the styler!
   "Jobs like tabernacles
   "Are what Bezaleel tackles.
"Oh, and death to each Sabbath-defiler!"

32
To a gold calf the people now bowed.
Angry Moses shrieked, "Death to this crowd!"
   The Levites complied:
   Three thousand men died.
"I'll get the rest later," God vowed.

33
"I'm not going with you lot," God whined.
Moses pleaded, and God changed his mind.
   They spoke face to face
   In that tent-temple place.
God Almighty showed Mo his behind.

34
Mo made the tablets anew.
(Broke the first ones in Ex 32.)
   God gamely constructs
   Commandments redux!
So happy was Mo, his face glew!

35
Now Moses told all he had seen
And called on all folk wise and keen
   To bring what they could
   And the temple make good.
(Like in *Witness*, that barn-building scene.)

36
Mo pronounced, "We have more than enough!
"If you ain't offered yet, it's just tough."
   Boards, curtains and sockets,
   All those flanges and sprockets!
Bez and co. set to work on the stuff.

37
Bezaleel made the ark, staves and rings,
Mercy seat beneath cherubim's wings;
   He made table and poles
   And dishes and bowls,
Altar, candlestick, sweet-smelling things.

38
One more altar, and vessels of brass,
And the court, where folks gather *en masse*.
   Point-six million gallants
   Gave one hundred talents
For that silver and gold touch of class.

39
Lastly garments for Aaron they made,
With yarn, jewels and gold, all top grade.
   They checked on the list:
   There was nothing they'd missed!
Moses blessed them for all he surveyed.

40
They assembled the parts they'd amassed.
The tabernacle was ready at last!
   Its environs were graced
   By God's presence (cloud-based).
Their march had to wait till He'd passed.

LEVITICUS

1
"Listen here, Mo, I want a fine spread
"When folks slaughter their best quadruped.
   "Burn unblemished males
   "Or the sacrifice fails.
"(But with doves, you just pull off their heads.)"

2
"Now, for bread, I'm no big fan of yeast,
"But I do want my muffins well-greased.
   "Plain cooking – naught funny.
   "Don't be burning up honey!
"And the bulk goes to fatten the priest."

Leviticus

3

"For a peace offering, you may deliver
"The organs, with fat, just a sliver.
    "Be it long understood:
    "Eat no fat or blood!
"As for me, I'll have kidneys with liver."

4

"If people screw up by mistake
"Then the usual bits they must bake.
    "For the masses, and priests,
    "Burn bullocks deceased.
"Kings and peasants, a goat they'll forsake."

5

"Silent witness, unclean or oath-taker:
"Offer lambs, kids or doves to your Maker.
    "If I'm trespassed against,
    "I must be recompensed
"With a whole ram, for such a lawbreaker."

6

"If you steal, give back a fifth more.
"Keep my altar alight, I implore.
    "Let the Aaronites eat
    "Some grain and some meat.
"Things are holy that contact the gore."

7

"Trespass offerings are like those for sin.
"The priest keeps the grain and the skin.
    "Don't eat stuff too late!
    "Fat and blood on no plate!
"Waves and heaves are for Aaron and kin."

8

Now Mo anoints Aaron and boys.
Two rams and a bull he destroys.
    He's no fuddy-duddy,
    For carnivores bloody
Are what Mo's tabernacle employs.

9

Two calves, bullock, kid, and some ram,
Topped with grain and some succulent lamb.
    Burn till well browned
    With blood spattered round.
(The one meat God don't like is ham...)

10

Two lads who had Aaron for sire
Came unto the Lord with strange fire.
    Nadab, Abihu,
    We bid you adieu!
Displease God and he'll burn you entire!

11

"Split-hoofed cud-munchers are fine.
"Must be both though: no camel or swine.
    "On no bugs that don't fly,
    "No crabs, octopi,
"No birds such as bats shall you dine!"

12

"When a woman gives birth to a daughter,
"Never mind all those towels and hot water!
    "Eighty days she is dirty!
    "(For a son, ten-and-thirty.)
"Send a lamb and a dove to the slaughter."

13

It seems that the priests are called in
For diagnosing diseases of skin.
    God dictates a process
    To Aaron and Moses,
But no cures are included therein.

14

"If a fellow's affliction soon ends,
"That fellow the priest must then cleanse.
    "The spell needs some toil
    "With blood, grain and oil,
"Three luckless lambs, and amens."

15

"Pus, women's menses, men's seed:
"All unclean, I presume we're agreed,
    "For a week in some cases.
    "Each time, offer braces
"Of doves." (Yet more bird deaths decreed...)

16

"In the seventh month on the tenth day,
"Procure goats, rams and bullock to slay.
    "On the chinny-chin-chin
    "Of one goat, hang your sin.
"In the wilds, send the damned thing away."

17
"Bring your dead critters up to the tent:
"The priests you must not circumvent.
  "Unshared sacrifice
  "Just adds to one's vice!
"Eat blood and you'll live to repent!"

18
"Don't get naked with any close kin,
"Or with beasts! Need I say it's a sin?
  "Man shan't lie with man!
  "It's not in the plan!
"Other tribes, they have no discipline!"

19
"Eat up your sacrifice quick!
"Don't wear linen with wool, that's just sick!
  "Trim no beards or crops.
  "Wait five years till fruit drops.
"Tup a slave, pay one ram for the trick!"

20
"Stone him who to Molech gives seed!
"Ditto wizards! Watch no woman bleed!
  "Curse ma and pa,
  "Or bed your wife's ma,
"Or adultery – die for the deed!"

21
"Blind, lame, scurvy, hump-backed or
                                stone-broke:
"Do not make a priest of that bloke!
  "Priests must marry a virgin
  "(They won't need much urgin'!),
"Stay indoors, and avoid all dead folk."

22
"Unclean priests shan't of holy things eat!
"For his kids, slaves and self is priest's meat.
  "When you slay sheep or goat
  "Or bullock, you ought
"To choose those that are well-formed and
                                neat."

23
"Holy is each convocation!
"Kill more critters, with routine cremation.
  "Unleavened bread,
  "All that stuff that I said.
"Dwell in booths, wave some leaves,
                                celebration!"

24
"Let Aaron look after my lamp!"
Meanwhile, some deuced cheeky scamp
  Blasphemed as he fought.
  God cried, "Let him be brought!
"Knock his block off with rocks outside
                                camp!"

25
"When you get there at last," God declared,
"Take each seventh year off. Be prepared
  "When no harvest grows.
  "After seven of those,
"Jubilee! All transgressions repaired."

26
"Obey, you'll have land, food and peace.
"Offend, and all good things shall cease:
  "Exile and ruin,
  "Whatever you're doin'!
"(Subject to my later caprice.)"

27
"A boy's worth a girl and a half.
"Have priests price up each offered calf.
  "For buy-back, augment
  "By twenty percent.
"Take tithes and beasts, on my behalf."

NUMBERS

1
"Call the twelve tribes to a rally!"
Six hundred thousand the tally
    Of men over twenty.
    "Let Levites stand sentry
Round the tent, lest strangers get pally."

2
"In the east camp Zeb, Izzy and Jude;
"South, Rube, Sim and Gad, all that brood;
    "West is Eph, Ben and Man,
    "North, Naph, Asher and Dan.
"Levite folk in the midst we exclude."

3
"Fold the curtains, ye west-camping Gershon.
"Fittings south, care of Kohath's exertion.
    "Firstborn fees to the priest,
    "Who camps in the east.
"Merarites bear north poles for insertion."

4
"With wrappings blue, purple and red,"
God told Mo, "wrap the plates and shewbread.
    "Hand all that to Kohath.
    "Now count, since you know math,
"Levite patriarchs!" "Eight thousand head!"

5
"Keep from camp the diversely defiled!
"Repay trespass to be reconciled!
    "A wife who's suspect
    "Drinks mud to be checked:
"If unfaithful, she'll ne'er bear a child."

6
"When the Nazarite vow one's professing,
"With corpses and grapes, no transgressing!
    "At the end, shave your head,
    "Leave a ram, two lambs dead.
"By the way, here's a general-use blessing."

7
For the temple's first day, from the flock
Twelve tribes slaughtered their finest livestock:
    Full two-fifty-two
    Beasts that went moo
Or bleated or baa'ed, on the block.

8
"I killed Egypt's kids way back when.
"You've owed me your firstborn since then,
    "So the Levites must wash
    "(And two bullocks kibosh):
"In their prime they'll be my temple-men."

9
"Passover! First month, fourteenth day.
"(For corpse-fondlers, next month is okay.)"
    Mo's folk up and went
    When God's cloud left the tent.
(Theological fog signalled "Stay!")

10
"Silver horns make a nice fire alarm!"
With a blast then set forth the whole farm
    (Though Mo's father-in-law,
    Hobab, wouldn't go).
"Tally-ho, God! Our enemies harm!"

11
God fried those who kvetched at camp's edge.
Cried Mo, "They want meat, fruit and veg!"
    God swept birds in a gale:
    "There, a month you'll eat quail!"
Then he plagued them – not quite as per pledge...

12
Aaron and sister complained:
"With Mo's new wife the family's stained!"
    "Aaron, for quibbling,
    "I've afflicted your sibling!
"Shut her out till her leprosy's waned."

13
Said God, "Check the lie of the land."
Mo heard from his top scouting band:
    "Many giants remain an'
    "Occupy Canaan!
"We're grasshoppers, wholly unmanned!"

14

The people cried, "Giants?! Let's scarper!"
God sulked, and plagued each captain carper:
    "No Canaan for you!"
    Those that tried to get through
Found Amalekite swords were the sharper.

15

"More offerings! Heave, slice and singe
"When you notice you've sinned and then cringe.
    "Who picks sticks on a Sunday,
    "Pelt with stones on the Monday!
"Think of me when you fondle your fringe."

16

Two-fifty rebelled with bold Korah.
An abyss gulped them out of the Torah!
    Thousands fourteen-point-seven
    Were flattened by Heaven
Before Aaron atoned with his aura!

17

"Here's a good one!" said God. "Get twelve sticks!
"Put 'em here in the temple and mix.
    "Now see Aaron's blossom!"
    The folks said, "That's awesome,
"But we're dying, enough with the tricks!"

18

"Temple fixers, those fine sons of Levi,
"Must mind manners, lest they and e'en ye die!
    "You priests and your buddies
    "Grow fat on the goodies.
"A tenth of each offering heave high."

19

God said, "Make up some red heifer potion.
"For those left unclean, it's a lotion,
    "A pure body-spread
    "After touching the dead.
"Without that, they're cast out from devotion!"

20

Mo saw no fix for folks' thirst.
God said, "Split the rock! And how durst
    "Thou doubt my intent?
    "For your tacit dissent
"No promised land! Aaron dies first!"

21

Once more did the folks bellyache.
They were plagued and then cured by a snake.
    They killed Og and Sihon,
    Took Hormah and Heshbon,
And a well of Beer gave them a break.

22

"Mo's mobbing Moab, man!" So moaned
Balak to Balaam. God postponed
    Balaam's trip. Said his ass:
    "Angel won't let me pass!"
'Laam told 'Lak, "I am God-chaperoned!"

23

Seven bulls and rams killed by Balak!
No doubt God enjoyed the hot snack,
    But He said, through Balaam,
    "I am what I am!
"I'm on Mo's side in any attack."

24

Though twice more were animals killed,
Balaam's words left Balak unfulfilled.
    "I asked you to curse!
    "You've just made things worse!"
Said Balaam: "Mo will win, as God willed."

25

"Hang their heads, they who worshipped Baalpeor!"
Strange women some took. God's severe.
    For one Midian "bride"
    Twenty-four thousand died.
Phinehas ran her through with a spear.

26

"Count again!" said God. Mo so arranged
With El'zar (for Aaron exchanged).
    There was hardly a guy
    From the time of Sinai,
But the numbers were largely unchanged.

27

"When it comes to whom stuff descends to,
"Sans sons, father's daughters will do.
  "Now your time is up, Mo!"
  "But who'll lead when I go?"
"Let young Joshua make his debut."

28

"Two lambs daily, with wine and some flour.
"At each Sabbath, two more I'll devour.
  "New month: seven lamb;
  "Two bulls; goat and ram.
"Same deal at each feast of my power."

29

"Even then, I'll be needing more gore:
"On the days that surround Yom Kippur
  "My appetite's keen:
  "Two-hundred-nineteen
"Lambs, rams, bullocks and goats are done for."

30

A man must respect his own oath,
But a woman is bound by her troth
  And the iron diktat
  Of by whom she's begat:
Dad and hubby can gainsay her, both.

31

Twelve thousand set off on crusades
And felled Midian kings with their blades.
  They slew to excess!
  (Mo leaves us to guess
What the priest did with thirty-two maids.)

32

Gad and Reuben sloped up looking smarmy.
"You want land?" spluttered Mo. "Think I'm barmy?!"
  "'Twas a war like *The Iliad*!
  "At least give us Gilead!"
"All right, but you're still in the army!"

33

There's a long list of places Mo went
With the Israelites, that blessèd tent.
  After travels and woes,
  Canaan's still full of foes.
"Drive 'em out, or have cause to repent!"

34

"Canaan should just drop in your lap.
"Here's the borders." God rolled out the map.
  "From Hor down to Zin.
  "At Egypt, curl in.
"Now, each chief, come and pick out a scrap."

35

"Lots of work for the Levite surveyor!
"Lay out cities, with some for the slayer.
  "He's safe when within
  "From revenge by mad kin.
"Without that he hasn't a prayer!"

36

Zelophahed's tribesfolk complained:
"We might lose all the land we've obtained!
  "When women inherit,
  "They go off and share it!"
"Marry cousins then," Moses ordained.

DEUTERONOMY

1

Mo recapped: "God offered you land!
"'Crush the Amorites!' was his command.
  "But you quibbled and quailed,
  "Fought without Him and failed.
"If only you'd done what He'd planned!"

2

"We passed lands of Esau and Lot,
"Till our rebels were dead and forgot.
  "We killed Heshbon's king
  "And each living thing!
"Took it all! (Except where we did not.)"

Deuteronomy

3

"We killed Og, of the Very Big Bed!
"Manny, Reuben and Gad picked their spread.
   "But I can't cross the brook,
   "I get only a look,
"And then Josh will grow wrath in my stead."

4

"Hark! I'll go over the law
"That ye heard from the mountain in awe!
   "God did lots of great stuff!
   "You can't worship enough!
"(But He's bashful: don't sculpt Him or draw.)"

5

"God gave us commandments!" cried Mo.
"And ye wailed, 'Ooh, He's scary! You go!'
   "So I did, and God said:
   "'**Good call. They'll be dead**
"'**If they wander from my status quo!**'"

6

Now, Moses can labour a point:
"Keep God's laws, and do not disappoint!
   "For the good Lord is jealous,
   "So listen up, fellas!
"Teach your kids to look after this joint!"

7

"Show no mercy when you go a-warring!
"After other gods don't go a-whoring!
   "God will give you good things
   "When you kill all their kings!"
(Mo's pep talk is tough, but it's boring.)

8

"This land up ahead has it all!
"God brought you here, always recall.
   "Four decades of manna!
   "What a catering planner!
"Don't let other gods hold you in thrall!"

9

"With God here, our foes we'll eject
"('Cause they're wicked – we're only stiff-necked)."
   Then Mo tells his stories –
   Tablets, old glories.
"Still and all, we're God's favourite sect!"

10

After more reminiscing from Moses:
"Keep the statutes that our God imposes!
   "For the Lord God is great
   "And He'll be your best mate!
"Just be true, and life's one bed of roses!"

11

"Remember what wonders we saw
"When from Egypt God helped us withdraw?
   "With this new real estate
   "Israel will be great!
"Did I mention to follow God's law?"

12

"When you're done being all homicidal,
"Demolish each altar and idol.
   "God will set out his stall:
   "Kill and eat, have a ball!
"But do not up to foreign gods sidle!"

13

"To kill a false prophet's no loss!
"Stone any that you come across.
   "If a city kowtows
   "To new gods, slash its cows,
"Burn it down, kill 'em all, it is dross!"

14

"Let's go over this clean-unclean thing.
"Eat no bats and no bugs on the wing.
   "The good Lord forbids
   "Any seething of kids!
"At tithe time, just eat what you bring!"

15

"In year seven, forgive in-group debt.
"Help the poor – you'll have no regret.
   "If a freed slave stays near,
   "Put a hole through his ear!
"Eat firstlings – not blood, don't forget!"

16

"Passover's month is Abib.
"Later, feast with each servant and sib:
   "Seven weeks from grain's chop,
   "And a week when you stop.
"Appoint judges to make law *ad lib*."

17

"They who worship the stars, moon and sun,
"Stone to death for the evil they've done!
    "(On two people's say-so.)
    "If two quarrel, well, heigh-ho,
"Let your judges and kings favour one."

18

"Levite priests eat the shoulder and face.
"Any Levite can take up his place.
    "Offer witches no praise,
    "Nor yet wizards! God says:
"'**MY PROPHETS WILL PUT THE TRUE CASE.**'"

19

"So the man of manslaughter might flee,
"Set aside in your lands cities three
    "(With three more to follow).
    "Lest justice be hollow,
"Smite false witness, a knee for a knee!"

20

"You've had house, wine and wife? You can fight!
"When besieging somewhere out of sight
    "Keep some slaves, be a sorter!
    "But in homelands – no quarter!
"For seigeworks, no fruity trees blight!"

21

"Fix a murder by killing a cow.
"Wed a captive until she says, '*Ciao!*'
    "Give the firstborn the bulk.
    "Stone a son in a sulk.
"Don't leave hanged men at night on the bough."

22

"Mind lost property! Never cross-dress!
"Don't mix ox, ass or fabric! Unless
    "In town screams are heard,
    "A girl's rape claim's absurd:
"With stones all such unions bless!"

23

"Bastards, keep out, for ten gens!
"Lovejuice and poo, quickly cleanse!
    "Give escaped slaves the nod.
    "Keep all vows made to God.
"Charge interest – but not to your friends."

24

"Don't remarry the one you divorced.
"No trading in Jews is endorsed!
    "Die for sins of your own.
    "Take no poor man's millstone.
"Leave some crops so the poor are resourced."

25

"Stop at forty when flogging: more mocks.
"Never muzzle a corn-treading ox.
    "Your bro's widow you'll wed,
    "Or go barefoot instead.
"Chop her hand, she who's crushed a man's rocks!"

26

"Bring a basket of fruit to the Lord;
"Tell the saga of Egypt, till bored.
    "From what falls to the scythe
    "Give the Levites your tithe.
"Keep God's laws, so we'll earn his reward."

27

"In Canaan, plaster laws on rough stone.
"Curse or bless, as befits your land zone.
    "Curse the idolatrist.
    "Curse who tups beast or sis.
"Curse each hitman, each killer unknown."

28

"All good things if you follow the rules;
"If not, God will punish you, fools,
    "With diseases and stuff.
    "He's a fiend in a huff:
"He'll turn you to babe-eating ghouls!"

29

"Listen up!" Moses cried, "Here's the deal,
"After Egypt and wars and ordeal:
    "You all can make hay
    "Till you worship astray,
"Then it's curses! That much He'll reveal."

30

"He'll disperse you, then gather you in,
"And love you once more – till you sin.
    "You know what He said!
    "Keep it all in your head!
"Cleave to the Lord, and you'll win!"

31

"Read out these laws to the throng!
"Though we all know you'll later do wrong.
　　"You'll be praying away –
　　"God won't half make you pay!
"But shut up now, I've written a song!"

32

"God is great!" (Moses sang) "But He's stern.
"You forsook God, and He you in turn.
　　"But he kind of relented,
　　"Disaster prevented.
"Keep His law, if long life you would earn."

33

"And now the big finish!" cried Mo.
"Bless Reuben, Jude, Lev, Ben and Jo!
　　"Zeb, Iss, Gad and Dan!
　　"Naph and Ash! God's a fan!"
(Not a word for poor Simeon though!)

34

After glimpsing what's on the far side
Of the mountain, poor Mo up and died.
　　His sepulchre's hid.
　　None has done what he did,
And the people of Israel cried.

JOSHUA

1

"**JOSH, YOU'RE UP!**" said God. "**GATHER YOUR CREW.**
"**GO TAKE CANAAN! THINK: WHAT WOULD MO DO?**"
　　So Josh cried, "Three days!
　　"Then our foes we'll amaze!"
The folks cheered: "Josh is Moses anew!"

2

To Jericho Josh sent his spies.
Rahab hid them from king's soldiers' eyes.
　　The grateful pair said,
　　"Hang up this scarlet thread:
"We'll spare you when everyone dies."

3

It was time to head off for the war!
God said, "**FOLLOW THE ARK TO THE SHORE!**"
　　At the Jordan, a priest
　　Toed the flow and it ceased!
(Wet sandals can be such a bore.)

4

Josh set souvenir stones in Gilgal
To remember the dried-up canal:
　　"Rocks from under the spate
　　"Are the proof God is great!
"Tell your children the whole rationale."

5

"**CUT THE FORESKINS OF THIS GENERATION!**"
No more manna – the end of migration.
　　Some fellow with sword
　　Led the host of the Lord.
Josh kicked off his shoes in prostration.

6

God said, "**HERE'S HOW TO CAST MY NEW SPELL:**
"**SEVEN LAPS, PRIESTS AND TRUMPETS – RAISE HELL!**"
　　So Josh blew the place down
　　And won his renown:
Rahab lived, but all Jericho fell.

7

Defeated at Ai! In chagrin,
Josh pinpointed the source of the sin:
　　"You stole Jericho's loot!"
　　Achan couldn't refute,
So they stoned and burned him and his kin.

8

With an ambush, Josh lifted his spear
And jabbed men of Ai in the rear.
　　Thousands slaughtered outright,
　　The king hanged until night.
Josh chiselled law on the frontier.

9

Where Josh goes, there everyone dies!
So Gibeonites came in disguise.
    "We're poor! Let us stay!
    "We're from far, far away!"
Josh harrumphed, notwithstanding their lies.

10

Josh fought gathered foes with a will.
Heavy hail! Sun and moon standing still!
    Five kings caved in!
    "Let the slaughter begin!"
Cities massacred, usual drill.

11

Hazor's king and the rest made a pact,
Yet 'twas not they but Josh who attacked.
    The chariots blazed,
    The cities were razed.
Ethnic cleansing left farmland intact.

12

Sure, Moses killed Og and Sihon,
But Josh slaughtered Ai and Hebron,
    Debir, Jericho,
    Arad, Megiddo...
To Mo's two, Josh slammed home thirty-one!

13

"You're old, Josh! Don't quibble, you are!
"But there's more land in Canaan's bazaar!
    "These bits went to Gad,
    "To Rube, and Jo's lad..."
(By now Josh felt older by far.)

14

They drew lots, and soon Caleb appeared:
"Recall *Numbers* 13, how folk feared
    "To tread here? But I
    "Said to give it a try!"
And so Hebron Cal now commandeered.

15

Judah's borders hauled in a fine catch:
Five score cities and more in one patch!
    On Jerusalem's folk
    Judah's warring wave broke:
In the Jebusites they met their match.

16

Land for the tribes of Jo's boys:
West of Jericho Ephraim deploys.
    The allocation committees
    Give his bro' half his cities!
Canaanites Ephraim keeps for his toys.

17

Mannaseh somehow won a huge tract
For their boys, or their girls where sons lacked.
    The bros form a cordon
    Both sides of the Jordan,
Promised Canaanite hills when they're sacked.

18

Seven tribes needed yet to take root.
They went to survey and compute.
    Thus the map would include
    Ben, betwixt Jo and Jude;
Jericho and Jerus'lem to boot!

19

Simeon's bit's inside of Jude's;
Naphtali's to Jordan extrudes.
    Zeb, Ash, Iss and Dan
    All get marked on the plan
And the slicing of Canaan concludes.

20

"Now let me remind you again
"About cities for those who have slain.
    "There a killer can wait
    "Till the priest meets his fate."
Josh picked six towns within God's domain.

21

Then the Levites came nagging, and so
Josh allotted them places to go.
    They got forty-eight towns
    And the land that surrounds.
At last Israel's status was quo!

22

Back home went Rube, Manny and Gad.
At the river an altar they add.
    The other tribes booed,
    But they cried: "It's not rude!
"It reminds all our kids of Big Dad!"

23

Said Joshua: "So listen, I ain't
"Long for this world. Show restraint!
    "Do what Moses said;
    "If you wander instead
"You'll be doomed, with no cause for complaint!"

24

"Abe, Jake, Isaac and Moses we knew.
"All this land for us God overthrew!
    "So serve God or regret it!"
    They groaned: "Yes, we get it."
Then Josh died – high priest Eleazar too.

JUDGES

1

Defeated by Jude, Sim and chums,
Ad'bezek was all fingers and thumbs.
    Many Canaanite races
    Endure in their places;
Each to Israel glumly succumbs.

2

Said God's angel: "Survivors? What gives?"
Josh's cohort now no longer lives.
    The new crew make God snarl:
    "They all worship Baal!"
Gives 'em judges; still judges, misgives.

3

The folks embrace strange gods and trees,
Oft in thrall, since their Lord they displease.
    King Eglon the hefty
    Falls to Ehud the lefty,
Then Moab the Israelites seize.

4

Said Debs: "Go beat Sisera's chariot,
"Barak, with ten thou' proletariat."
    Heber's wife Jael
    Put first milk, then a nail
In Sisera – minxy Iscariot!

5

Debs and Barak then sang a duet
(Released only, back then, on cassette),
    Praising soldiers and God,
    Dissing Sisera's squad.
Decades' peace for this war minuet.

6

To prove him the man to fight Midian,
God cooked up the mutton of Gideon.
    Gid tore down Baal's shrine,
    Brought the tribes into line.
God moistened Gid's fleece: **"Now get rid of 'em!"**

7

Giddy's first requisite in his troops
Is: take no man who for his drink stoops.
    Convinced by some oaf
    Who dreamed of a loaf,
He blew Zeeb's and Oreb's heads off – oops!

8

Gid flattered Ephraim. Wanted buns!
Killed Zebah, Zalmunna and chums.
    No succour from Succoth!
    Their princes he struketh!
Left gold earrings and seventy sons.

9

Sixty-nine souls at Abi's hand died.
Little Jotham cursed: "Thorn in my side!"
    By Gaal galled, Abi burned
    Those of Shechem who'd turned.
Killed by sword after stone crushed his pride.

10

Tola and Jair and his asses
Led. Now they're dead. Each man passes!
    The people's faith failed
    And Ammon prevailed.
"He who's barmy in Gilead, beat these masses!"

11

Whoreson Jephthah they chose for the slaughter.
His triumph was priceless! Well, sorta:
    He made God an oath
    That he'd burn what came forth
To greet him. Aw, shucks, 'twas his daughter!

JUDGES

12

Next, Ephraim came grumbling around.
Jephthah won, but some sought common ground.
    "Your shibboleth's fake!
    "You'll rue that mishtake!"
Thousands died for a sibilant sound.

13

Three more judges, then people went bad.
Said an angel, "You'll soon be a dad!"
    Manoah thought it a joke
    Till he went up in smoke!
Soon came Samson, a fine hairy lad.

14

On the way to his Philistine squeeze,
The lion Sam killed filled with bees.
    His wife's pig-in-the-middle
    When her friends try his riddle.
Sam leaves her. Killed thirty, this wheeze!

15

For his handed-down wife, Sam burns wheat.
In revenge, her folks burn her complete!
    In their midst, tied and thrown,
    Sam bursts forth with a bone,
Kills a thousand, then drinks water neat.

16

Delilah nags until poor Samson's will is
Worn down. He admits his Achilles'
    Heel's his hair's length.
    Shaved, he grows back his strength,
Blindly brings down the house on the Phillies!

17

Micah said, "Take this silver back, Mum."
"All for God!" she cried. ('All' here means 'some'.)
    A Levite soon called.
    Micah had him installed
As his priest. "Now the Lord is my chum!"

18

Short of land, the Danites made a plan;
Sent spies to survey, then began:
    They took Micah's god,
    His priest and ephod,
Took the town, and of course called it Dan.

19

In Gibeah a Levite pair stayed.
Folks cried: "Give us your guest to degrade!"
    The Levite's wife died
    When he sent her outside.
In twelve parts she was widely conveyed.

20

Bits of wife across Israel came.
Vengeful tribes at Gibeah took aim.
    As their wrath was fulfilled
    Sixty thousand were killed,
And the Benjamite towns set aflame.

21

But the Benjamite tribe will now fade!
So Jabesh is scourged, but for each maid.
    The Benjamites lie low,
    Snatch dancers from Shiloh.
They got screwed, but at least they'll get laid!

RUTH

1

Husbands died, leaving Orpah and Ruth.
Ma said, "Go, gals! I'm long past my youth.
    "No more sons you can wed."
    Ruth tarried instead,
And "God hates me!" wailed Ma. "That's the truth!"

2

Ruth went gleaning for barley and wheat.
Kinsman Boaz said, "Well done! Now eat.
    "You can harvest my field
    "For all it will yield."
Cooed Naomi, her Ma, "Ain't he sweet?"

3

"Warm the feet of Boaz!" ordered Ma.
He found Ruth lying there; cried, "Aha!
    "We'll soon see you right.
    "Go now while it's night."
She brought home more barley, hurrah!

4

One kin to Boaz hedged his bets,
Wouldn't marry Ruth; so, with regrets,
    Passed him land, wife and shoe.
    Without further ado,
David's line on Ruth Boaz begets.

1 SAMUEL

1

Off to sacrifice goes good Elkanah.
Wife Peninnah picks on wife Hannah.
    Hannah prays for a child
    In a manner most mild:
Sam's the answer to Hannah's hosanna.

2

Hannah sang, and Sam worked for the priest,
Eli, whose sons were well greased.
    God grumbled, **"THEY'LL PAY**
    "FOR GOING ASTRAY.
"IT'S A DAMNED SHAME YOUR SONS WEREN'T POLICED!"

3

"I'm sleeping, Eli," grumbled Sam.
"IT'S ME, GOD! THE BIGGEST 'I AM'!
    "ELI'D BETTER WATCH OUT!"
    So Sam spread it about,
Just like that, instant prophet, wham-bam!

4

Fighting Phillies were riding roughshod.
Eli's lads brought the tablets of God,
    At a terrible cost –
    Both sons and ark lost!
Eli died, but grandsired Ichabod.

5

Philistines took the ark to Ashdod.
It beheaded poor Dagon, their god.
    The nuisance passed on
    To Gath and Ekron.
"Send it back, we've all got emerods!"

6

"Make gold haemorrhoids!" [Possibly 'tumours'?]
"And gold mice, to assuage God's ill humours!"
    So the Phils, playing smart,
    Sent ark, idols and cart
Back home to their rightful consumers.

7

When the ark returned, two decades passed
With the Israelites sorely outclassed.
    Sam said, "Worship the Lord
    "And we'll see off this horde!"
Thus the Philistines fled them at last.

8

Sam's sons judged, but each proved a knave.
Said the folks, "Look, a king's what we crave!"
    So God shrugged, and Sam said,
    "Be it on your own head!
"For a king will make each man a slave."

9

Saul and servant met Sam on the passes.
"I'm a seer," said Sam. "Saw your asses!
    "Saul, you're our lucky winner!
    "A nice joint for dinner,
"And God's picked you to rule o'er the masses!"

10

Some chaps gave a sandwich to Saul.
(Clever Sam had predicted it all.)
    He turned into a prophet.
    The folks cried, "Come off it!"
But he soon had all Israel in thrall.

11

Nahash warned, "I'll have your right eyes!"
Angry Saul chopped his ox down to size:
    "Your oxen are next!"
    So cowed people, much vexed,
Killed and scattered those Ammonite guys.

12

Cried Sam, "D'y'all recollect when..?"
(The folks groaned: "Not Egypt again!")
    "Observe, for a wonder,
    "Some unlikely thunder!
"Henceforth, act like good godly men!"

13

Saul prepared for a Philistine clash
By burning his offering to ash.
    Sam complained, "'Twas ill done!
    "Now your prospects are gone!"
So Saul's left in a right old Michmash!

14

Saul's lad Jon ran by rocks on a raid.
Killed a score! ('Twas good luck he'd a blade!)
    But the sweet taste of honey
    Proved a sin for Saul's sonny.
Still, on Phillies and foes Saul's men preyed.

15

God said, "**Wipe out the Amalek species!**"
Sheepish Saul spared some milkers and fleeces.
    Sam cried, "*J'accuse!*
    "I hear bleating and moos!"
Saul's dethroned; King Agag goes to pieces.

16

Saul-sick, God sends in the new wave:
"**Anoint Jesse's eighth son, shepherd Dave!**"
    Sam found the young pup
    And oiled him up.
Saul's sick soul's soothed by harp songs Dave gave.

17

The Philistines' champ, Big Goliath
Cried, "If you think you're hard, come and trieth!"
    Dave's slyly-slung stone
    Broke the big brute's headbone.
Spluttered Saul, "Who's this stripling I spieth?"

18

Jonny loved Dave, but Saul couldn't.
He sighed, "Marry my girls!" But Dave wouldn't.
    For bride-price, Saul's will is
    Five-score foreskins of Phillies.
Dave pays, but Saul hates him. He shouldn't!

19

At Jon's word, King Saul took Dave back,
Launched an unprovoked javelin attack!
    From this quaint peccadillo,
    David fled, left a pillow.
Saul rolled naked on Samuel's track.

20

Dave hides, and will not come to tea.
Jon explains, "Look, he asked leave of me."
    "He still should be here!"
    Saul cries, flinging a spear.
So Jon's arrows steer young Dave to flee.

21

"It's a mission from Saul!" David said;
Thus blagged from Nob's priest blade and bread.
    Lest it might be the wish
    Of Gath's king, Achish,
That Dave died, he played wrong-in-the-head.

22

Dave drew four-hundred-plus malcontents.
Saul bawled, "Whence come these dissents?"
    Saul's Doeg killed the priest;
    All of Nob soon deceased,
Barring one, who with Dave waits events.

23

The Phillies at Keilah Dave beat.
Saul chased him, and Dave felt the heat.
    Not there could he stay on,
    Nor in Ziph, nor in Maon,
But the Philistines forced Saul's retreat.

24

While Saul took a dump in Engedi,
Dave's mates whispered, "Kill him, get ready!"
    Dave cut only Saul's skirt:
    "See, I mean you no hurt!"
So they parted: their friendship looked steady.

25

Sam died! Nabal gave Dave no food.
His wife was appalled: "He's so rude!"
    When David saw red
    She brought him a spread.
Nabal died, and Dave Abigail wooed.

1 Samuel

26

Saul worried, and sought Dave in Ziph.
Dave waved Saul's spear from a cliff:
    "Look, I spared you again!
    "Let's be sensible men!"
Saul agreed, ending this latest tiff.

27

Dave hid with Achish o'er in Gath.
Still killed Phillies – some chutzpah he hath!
    He claimed that his fights
    Were with Israelites,
Led Achish down the wrong bloodied path.

28

Since God wouldn't speak to him, Saul
Told a witch, "Call up those in your thrall!"
    The dread shade of Samuel
    Intoned, "God'll damn you all!"
(But beef sandwich will sorrow forestall.)

29

The Philistines mustered. But wait!
There's Dave in the back! "Listen, mate,
    "You're not with us. Go!"
    Achish sighed: "Make it so."
And they marched without Dave to their fate.

30

Dave's home-from-home, Ziklag, was burned!
God said, **"Go retrieve what you've earned!"**
    So Dave's crew benights
    Doomed Amalekites.
Loot's divided when all is returned.

31

Day of battle! Soon Saul's sons subside.
Arrow-pricked, sword inside, sad Saul died.
    The city-folk scarper.
    (No sign of the harper!)
Headless Saul's pin-up's pulled down and fried.

2 SAMUEL

1

This Amalekite's tale is disjointed:
Says 'twas *he* killed the king God anointed!
    Dave accepted the crown
    But then struck the wretch down,
His hopes of Dave's love disappointed!

2

"Go be Judah's king now!" David did.
But Abner crowned Saul's other kid.
    At the pool some swapped swords.
    Men fought for their lords.
Hundreds dead before David got rid.

3

Six sons had Dave. Ab took leave
Of Saul's son. Dave quibbled: "Retrieve
    "Michal, my wife!"
    But Joab took Ab's life.
"Not my fault!" cried Dave. "Let's all grieve."

4

Saul's son Ishbosheth had captains two,
Baan and Rech, and their liege-lord they slew.
    They took off his head,
    Galumphed back; but Dave said:
"Baand of Reches! The chop-block for you!"

5

So now David was Israel's leader.
Hiram built him a house made of cedar.
    He took Philistine lives
    And with girlfriends and wives
He had many more kids – a fast breeder!

6

Uzzah died when the loose ark he steadied.
At arm's length, a like fate Dave dreaded,
    But he hailed it with dancing.
    Michal scorned his prancing.
She was childless, howe'er often bedded!

7

Dave has plans: "A nice house for the ark!"
God snorts: **"I need no such bulwark,**
   "But Dave's boy can build it."
   "Let it be as God willed it!"
Cried Dave. "He's a fine patriarch!"

8

Phils and Moabs, with ropey technique,
David killed, and lots more of that clique.
   For God he'd amass
   Gold, silver and brass.
His career had achieved a new peak!

9

Had all Saul's kin met with their death?
David searched, and found Mephibosheth.
   "Here's Saul's land back complete!
   "Though you've got wobbly feet,
"You'll eat with me while you draw breath!"

10

Nahash died. His son, cheeky Hanun,
Bared cheeks, high and low, all for fun,
   Of King David's men,
   But regretted it when,
Fighting him and his Syrians, Dave won.

11

Bathsheba, she bathed and Dave boiled.
She came in; they were quickly embroiled.
   He sent Uri to die,
   Married Bathy thereby,
But his record with God was now spoiled.

12

"Rich in sheep, you stole Uriah's lamb!"
Nate chastised. "Now your son God'll damn!"
   Bathsheba's babe copped it:
   No prayers could have stopped it.
She bore Solomon next - thank you, ma'am!

13

Dave's son Amnon raped Tamar, his sis.
Her bro' Absalom took it amiss.
   His servants then smote
   That malingering goat.
Abs fled, but Dave soon forgave this.

14

Joab's words through a wise woman's throat
Shamed David to act as he ought.
   The King, though still wary,
   Took back Abs, cute and hairy.
Abs burned wheat, for Dad's blessing he sought.

15

For years Abs glad-handed the tribes;
Thence to Hebron. "We don't like the vibes,"
   Dave's counsellors said.
   Dave told Hush as they fled,
"Go spy on what plans Abs describes!"

16

Mephi stayed, Ziba claimed, with high hopes.
Shimei pelted Dave from the slopes.
   "Let him be," said Dave, sighing.
   Hushai commenced spying.
With Dad's girlfriends Abs wriggles and gropes.

17

Ahithophel told Abs, "Go tonight!"
But Hushai counselled, "Put off this fight!"
   Ahi, spurned, was suspended.
   Abs and David contended,
But three chaps brought Dave's people a bite.

18

Came the fight, and a thousand score died.
Oak boughs forked up Abs from his ride.
   Joab stabbed as Abs dangled.
   In a pit he was mangled.
'Twas the King's son withal, and Dave cried.

19

Joab grumbled 'cos Dave was depressed,
Still, Dave's gracious to all who transgressed:
   He forgave shamed Shimei,
   Eased Mephi's dismay,
Crossed the Jordan; but still met unrest.

20

Sheba blared, "We don't owe David jack!"
So David sent Joab to attack.
   A woman of Abel
   Foreshortened this fable
And Sheba: Joab took his head back.

21

'Cos Saul slaughtered Gibeon, God sent
Three years of famine. (Top gent!)
    Seven men of Saul's line
    Died twirling on twine,
But their bones to Saul's sepulchre went.

22

Dave bursts into song: "God's my shield!
"He snorts smoke above my battlefield!
    "In the darkness his light
    "Finds me out, as upright,
"And makes strangers and enemies yield."

23

Dave's last words: "God spoke unto me,
"Said, 'BE JUST!' Gave me all things for free!
    "Bad guys be dismissed!"
    Then we go on to list
His generals: top thirty, top three.

24

Grumpy God told Dave, **"HAVE THE TRIBES NUMBERED!"**
Then promptly with plague they were lumbered.
    On some bloke's threshing-floor
    Dave entreated, "No more!"
With burnt oxen God's wrath at last slumbered.

1 KINGS

1

The old King was warmed by a maid.
The throne was meanwhile claimed by Ade.
    But the crown went to Solomon,
    Saying, "Go tell this hollow man
"If he's good he need not be afraid."

2

"Pay back Ade, soldier Joab and Shimei,"
Dave said, dying. Sol didn't delay.
    "Could I please have Dave's maid?"
    Well, that did for young Ade.
Joab went next. Shimei died when astray.

3

Wedding Egypt's princess while he built,
Sol dreamed under Gibeon's quilt
    That God made him wise.
    So when harlots told lies,
Their moot babe he saved, no blood spilt.

4

And Sol set up princes and chiefs
With priests, scribes and regional briefs.
    At last peace was found
    And folks came from all round
To hear Sol expound his beliefs.

5

"How's it going?" asked Hiram of Tyre.
"Just the man!" cried Sol. "What I require
    "Is oodles of cedar!
    "In turn, we'll be your feeder."
Thousands laboured on King Sol's desire.

6

So this temple would be the Lord's seat.
Wood-faced stone, 'twas in length ninety feet.
    With tall cherubs, twofold,
    'Twas all finished in gold
And it took seven years to complete.

7

For himself and his wife Sol builds halls.
For more temple fittings he calls.
    There's brassworks from Hiram
    (For he knew how to fire 'em),
And the treasures of Dave Sol installs.

8

The ark was installed, and Sol spake:
"Dear God, don't your people forsake!"
    Six score thousand beasts
    Were slaughtered. Then feasts
For a fortnight, just mutton and steak!

9

God liked his new digs. "But obey!"
Sol gave junk towns to Hiram, as pay.
    Foreign folks he enslaved;
    His made sure they behaved.
His ships found gold – anchors aweigh!

10

Sheba's queen brought Sol riches and spice.
His kingdom was nigh paradise,
    For his ships brought fine trees,
    Apes and peacocks to please.
He'd a throne and he swapped merchandise.

11

With one thousand sweethearts, Sol's drawn
To worship their gods, not his own.
    "Your kingdom, it goes!"
    Snarled the Lord, raising foes.
Sol died wise, but he could not atone.

12

Rehoboam's now monarch, Sol's son.
Folks grumbled: "King Sol was a Hun!
    "Be gentler!" But no.
    So Rehob had to go.
King Jerry's gold calves show he's won.

13

"One-handed false worship is shameless,
"King Jerry!" warned a godly man, nameless.
    Said an interested prophet,
    "Here's bread, man, come scoff it!"
Fooled and filled, lion-killed, nigh-on blameless!

14

"God's evil on Israel and Jerry!
"You're his wife! Hurry home now to bury
    "The King's son Abijah,"
    Predicted Ahijah.
Rehob's Jerry's doomed adversary.

15

Judah's Abijam's bad. Things improved:
Of Asa his son God approved.
    Israel's rasher,
    Serving Nadab and Baasha.
But the high places were not removed.

16

Per the words of Jehu, Baasha died.
Son Elah, dead drunk - homicide!
    Zimri killed him, then fell
    To Omri. "Jezebel!"
Cried Ahab, next King: "Be my bride!"

17

"Ahab, reign without rain!" said Elijah.
Said God, "Ravens and widows provide ya
    "With water and bread!"
    But the widow's son's dead!
Eli brings him back to oblige 'er.

18

"Announce my return, Obadiah!"
Said Eli, and arranged trial by fire.
    Baal's prophets were spurned,
    While Eli's bullock burned.
The rain came. "Let's all go somewhere drier!"

19

Baalish Jezebel threatened Eli.
"Well, I'll flee to the hills and not die!"
    Said God, "For the land
    "Crown new kings, and in hand
"Take Elisha" - who put his yoke by.

20

"Give me all, Ahab!" cried Benhadad.
This demand made the King and God mad.
    In the hills and the plain
    Six score thousand were slain.
But the King let Ben go - very bad!

21

"My vineyard is mine!" said Naboth.
Ahab sulked. Jez his wife stirred God's wrath:
    "I've had Naboth stoned:
    "Now the vineyard's state-owned!"
God let Ahab live, in sackcloth.

22

Ahab fought beside Jehoshaphat;
Took an arrow, bled out, that was that.
    Ahaziah reigned next,
    Worshipped Baal; God was vexed;
While Jehoram on Judah's throne sat.

2 KINGS

1
Now Ahaz fell through his bedroom floor.
Said Elijah, "You shan't rise no more!"
    Ahaz wasn't thrifty:
    Twice sent Eli fifty,
Whom God burned when they came to implore.

2
Said Elisha, "Let me be like you."
Eli shrugged, and to heaven he blew.
    Elish split Jordan's spate.
    When kids jeered at his pate
He sent bears to tear up forty-two.

3
'Gainst Moab, Ahab's son formed a quorum:
Jehoshaphat, Edom, Jehoram.
    Elisha's wet trench
    With blood seemed to drench
The earth: Moab fled, no decorum.

4
Widow's debts paid with infinite oil!
Her son re-wrapped in his mortal coil!
    Just twenty loaves fed
    A hungry hundred!
Poison can't make Elisha's stew spoil!

5
To Naaman the leper's request
To be healed, Elish said, "Get undressed!
    "A swim's what you need!"
    His servant, for greed,
With disease, as with silver, was blessed.

6
Axes float! And Ben's troops are struck blind.
Could be killed by the King, but he's kind.
    But renewed siege by Ben
    Leads to eating children.
Cried the King: "Prophet's neck be redlined!"

7
"Cheap food here tomorrow, I say!"
Cried Elisha. A lord answered, "Nay!"
    But Ben's people had fled.
    All the Israelites fed
And trampled the lord in the clay.

8
Reborn son's ma skipped famine, returned.
Hazael said, "Ben's sick, I'm concerned!"
    "But you'll take his last breath,
    "Waterboard him to death!"
Elish wept for the wars he discerned.

9
The crown now to Jehu transfers.
"No peace while your ma Jez still errs!"
    He yells to Joram;
    Spikes the ruler quondam.
Jezzie fell, to be eaten by curs.

10
Ahab's seventy sons lost their head.
Chums of Ahaz, forty-two were left dead.
    Jehu also slew all
    The servants of Baal,
"But keep Jerry's gold calves," Jehu said.

11
Since Jehu'd killed Ahaz, now his mother
Killed all Judah's heirs – sister, brother...
    But Jehoash, long saved,
    Slew his grandma, depraved,
And was Judah's new King – yet another.

12
For twenty years, priests kept the loot,
But once handled by men of repute
    The Lord's house was mended;
    But Jehoash was ended:
Gave the gold away, given the boot.

13
Two more kings pass in Israel's land.
Jehoash (not him) learns what's planned:
    With a firm arrow's flight
    He beats Syria's might.
Bones of Elish still make dead men stand.

14

Post-Jehoash, Judah gets Amaziah,
And later his son Azariah.
    Much evil is done,
    Cities lost, cities won,
And Israel picks Zachariah.

15

Azariah, old leper, dies, as
Judah gets Joth and Ahaz.
    Shallum takes Israel,
    Menahem on his tail.
Pekahiah, Pek low, all that jazz.

16

Ahaz has a thing for strange gods:
Burns incense, his son, odds and sods.
    Pekah judged him inferior,
    But Ahaz hired Assyria.
Temple fittings he rides o'er roughshod.

17

Assyria shut up Hoshea,
Emptied all Israel but for Judea.
    They dumped them by Gozan;
    Not what they'd have chosen.
"**SHOULD'VE LISTENED!**" raged God the doomsayer.

18

Mo's snake and high places Hez smashed!
To pay off Assyria, he trashed
    The temple's fine treasures,
    But in vain were such measures:
They came back, left his envoys tongue-lashed.

19

In dismay, with rent clothes, Hezekiah
Took comfort from fiery Isaiah.
    God slaughtered nine score
    Of their thousands. Done for
Was their King and his made-up messiah.

20

Isaiah slapped fig on a boil:
Cured Hez, made the shadows recoil.
    Hez showed his fine things
    To the Babylon Kings,
Heard they'd later make off with the spoil.

21

Mannaseh worshipped gods that weren't real:
Idols, groves, burned his son, the whole deal.
    "**REVENGE!**" vowed the Lord,
    But his protest's ignored:
Amon's next, and he's less than ideal.

22

A well-meaning King is Josiah.
Heard the words of the Lord from Hilkiah.
    A prophetess said:
    "Our despair lies ahead,
"But don't fret, before then you'll expire!"

23

So Joe brought the people in line,
Killed the priests, threw the junk from the shrine.
    God barked, "**I'M STILL MAD!**"
    Next, Jehoahaz was bad,
Then Eliakim paid Pharaoh's fine.

24

Jehoiachin's the next name.
Babylon's Nebuchadnezzar came,
    Took all the best folk,
    Put them under the yoke.
Zedekiah was crowned, much the same.

25

But Neb besieged Zed, killed his lads,
Took his eyes, took his brass and comrades.
    Jerusalem's razed.
    The Lord's temple blazed.
Back to Egypt! Once more they're nomads.

1 CHRONICLES

1

Here's a long list of dads with their boys,
From Adam to Edom: such joys!
    Perusing odd names
    And family-tree games,
The whole thing blurs into white noise.

1 Chronicles

2

More names: first the twelve sons of Jake,
Then Jude, and the lines his sons make.
    You'll miss, if you're skimmin',
      King Dave, and the women,
But at least you might still stay awake!

3

The descendants of David the King!
Sixty sons in that line – quite a string
    (Only two daughters listed –
      More must have existed!),
Almost all from Dave's Bathsheba fling.

4

Random glimpses of Judah's line next,
Disjointed to leave us perplexed.
    For Jabez, things went well,
      And for Simeon, swell,
But it's quite a bewildering text.

5

Next the offspring of Reuben and Gad,
Scattered in and around Gilead.
    With half Mannaseh
      These tribes won the day
Against Hag'rites, but then they went bad.

6

From the Levites come Aaron and Moses:
Endless priests, until King Neb forecloses,
    So Jehozadak's last.
      For Dave's choir, here's the cast,
And then towns of which Israel disposes.

7

We go on with the family tree,
And it's Iz, Ben and Naph's pedigree;
    Ash and Mannaseh then:
      It's all valorous men,
But for Ephraim's cow-rustling spree.

8

More on Ben and his sons, a new list
That markedly differs. The gist
    Is that of him came Saul
      And that's about all.
Ulam's seed, if not bow, rarely missed.

9

This chapter sets out to disclose
How Ben's offspring, and Judah's, and Jo's
    In Jerusalem were,
      And what they did there:
Mainly polish the props for priests' shows.

10

Saul set up his sword, fell upon,
And was hung in the shrine of Dagon.
    His sons were killed too.
      (None of this will sound new,
'Cos it recaps 1 Sam 31.)

11

"Let David be King!" cry the folks.
Then the Jebusites David provokes.
    Joab is his colonel,
      With his thirty fraternal
Men of arms, topped by three mighty blokes.

12

Soldiers joined Dave at Ziklag.
At Hebron more flocked to his flag.
    Of asses and cows and
      Some three hundred thousand
Supporters King David could brag.

13

"Let's gather the rest, and the ark!"
On this holy cart trek they embark.
    Uzza steadies the crate
      And at once meets his fate.
So Dave stows it: "Enough of this lark!"

14

Hiram sent David some wood.
David saw that his kingdom was good.
    He had lots of kids
      And the Philistines' bids
To defeat him he blithely withstood.

15

Priests and Levites take hold of the staves;
The ark travels on musical waves.
    With cymbals and singing,
      The procession is swinging!
Saul's Michal hates those dances of Dave's.

1 Chronicles

16

In the tent of the ark Dave burnt beasts,
Dealt out bread, meat and wine for the feasts.
　　"The Lord is our balm!"
　　He sang in a psalm.
The ark stayed with Zadok and his priests.

17

"Would you like a new house, God?" Dave said.
"I'll be fine for now out in the shed.
　　"Let Solomon do it.
　　"Now don't misconstrue it:
"By your line shall this land e'er be led."

18

Twenty-two kilo-Syrians died
At Dave's hand; men of Edom beside,
　　Eighteen thousands of them;
　　And from out the mayhem,
With treasures the temple's supplied.

19

Hanun shaved, showed and shamed Dave's
　　　　　　　　　　　　　　consolers.
He forgot that he messed with a brawler!
　　The Syrians fled –
　　Forty-seven-k dead –
Bent the knee to King Dave, holy roller.

20

Dave's a talent for taking a crown:
He and Joab razed the Ammonite's town.
　　Three sons of Gath's giant,
　　Bellicosely defiant,
Were by King David's men taken down.

21

Said Satan, "Go count all your men!"
There were 1.5 million by then –
　　Seven ten-thousands less
　　Through God's plague. "I confess!"
David cried. God repented again.

22

King Dave laid up building material
For son Sol, who's the next big imperial:
　　Gold, silver and woods,
　　The finest of goods
For the house of the Lord God ethereal.

23

Thirty-eight thousand Levites Dave polled.
Those past thirty (or twenty?) years old
　　Would burn, bake and sift,
　　Would stand, pray and shift,
In the temple. "Don't groan, you're enrolled!"

24

Sixteen chief men from Eleazar,
Eight more from his bro' Ithamar.
　　So which man did what
　　Was chosen by lot.
Scribe Shemaiah's the priests' registrar.

25

More family listings, verbose.
For a place in the band, the fight's close,
　　So two-hundred-eight-eight
　　Drew lots, to play straight.
We won't name 'em, the list is too gross.

26

Gatekeeping's a duty and pleasure.
Merari and Kore had the measure:
　　The small and the great
　　Cast lots for each gate.
Shelomith's in charge of the treasure.

27

Every month twenty-four thousand men
Took their turn in the army. For ten
　　Of the tribes, chiefs are named
　　(Gad and Asher unclaimed!).
Heads of beasts, wine and trees appear then.

28

"Because I've been in the odd brawl,"
Grumbled David, "I can't build God's hall.
　　"It's Solomon's chore.
　　"Here's what is called for:
"Silver, gold and submission, that's all."

29

Said Dave, "Well, I've stored all this stuff
"For the temple, but still not enough."
　　His folks swelled the hoard,
　　Sang and killed for the Lord.
God brought Sol, the new king, up to snuff.

2 CHRONICLES

1
Where Dave was a sweet serenader,
His son Sol is a thoughtful persuader.
    A thousand beasts charred
    To win God's regard,
And wise Sol's soon a canny horse-trader.

2
Sol picked workers, a hundred and fifty
Thousand, to build up his nifty
    House for the Lord;
    Asked Hiram for board,
Paid in goods - not the time to be thrifty!

3
Dave saw God at Ornan's threshing-floor.
There Sol set up the temple's front door,
    With pillars we know as,
    Right, Jachin, left, Boaz,
Golden fittings and gemstones galore.

4
A brass altar and a brass ox-borne sea;
For the pillars, some fruit filigree.
    Doors of brass and gold plate,
    Every vessel ornate.
(For the goldsmith's, it's Sol's jubilee!)

5
When Sol made the Lord God's house proud,
Countless livestock were killed. Trumpets loud
    Celebrated the ark
    Which at long last could park
'Neath the cherubs. God purred in a cloud.

6
On opening day, Sol made a speech:
"God of Dave, will you please forgive each
    "Varied way we transgress
    "When we turn and confess?
"Let us off for this house, I beseech!"

7
God barbecued sacrificed beasts.
A thousand gross died. Then the feasts:
    All were happy and fed.
    "NICE TEMPLE," God said.
"STICK WITH ME AND I'LL LISTEN, AT LEAST."

8
Twenty years, and the temple was made.
Sol set up some cities and prayed.
    He housed Pharaoh's daughter,
    Maintained daily slaughter.
From Ophir lots of gold was conveyed.

9
Sheba's queen brought Sol wealth, got her fix
Of wisdom, and left her spice mix.
    With tribute and trade
    Golden wonders he made,
Gold talents per year: six-six-six.

10
Rehoboam: Sol's son's the new king;
Tells Jerry, "I'm the scorpion's sting!
    "I'll keep you in line!"
    The folks growled, "Fine!
"All your pedigree don't mean a thing!"

11
Fled to Judah, Reho fortified
Many towns 'gainst the deadly divide:
    His side of the feud:
    Ben, Levi and Jude,
Seventy-eight wives and girlfriends beside.

12
The ways of the Lord they forsook.
Egypt's army came north, and they took
    All Sol's golden shields.
    Reho knelt and appealed.
God forgave. (More in Shemaiah's book.)

13
Reho died; his son Abijah ruled.
Jeroboam brought forth Israel, tooled.
    "You're godless!" Ab cried.
    Half a million died,
Jerry too, having been ridiculed.

2 Chronicles

14

Ab's son Asa was eager to keep
To God's ways: whence a decade of sleep.
    Ethiopia came,
    But they lost their war game:
Asa won, ravaged towns, took their sheep.

15

Azariah said, "Trust in God!"
At Jerusalem gathered the squad.
    Seven thousand sheep burned.
    Toward God they all yearned.
Ma's false idol true Asa downtrod.

16

By Baasha was Asa assailed;
Called on Syria's Ben, and prevailed.
    Said the seer, "A war
    "Is what trust in God's for!"
By bad feet and bad faith, King's curtailed.

17

Jehoshaphat's next, godly man:
Spread the Word throughout all Judahstan.
    From his neighbours he'd reap
    Goats, silver and sheep.
Kept a million men, lest war began.

18

"Ramothgilead will fall!" Ahab's told,
But Micaiah says, "Don't be so bold."
    The Syrians left
    Jeho, but they cleft
Ahab's armour; he died as foretold.

19

Home chastised and chastened, Jeho
Raised up judges and priests: "Listen, though:
    "God's law circumscribes
    "Any bias or bribes.
"You're acting for Him here below."

20

Ammon armies! Jeho's in a funk.
God sends 'em berserk – a slam-dunk!
    Jeho's three days in looting
    The self-executing.
Joins with Ahaz – bad move – his ship's sunk.

21

Jehoram's King next; kills each rival;
So God, wanting Dave's line's survival,
    His bowels destroyed.
    The people enjoyed
His departure more than his arrival.

22

Jeho died at forty; his son,
Forty-two when his reign was begun,
    Bad Ahaz, fought Jehu,
    Who him and his slew.
His heirs his ma killed, all but one.

23

Little Joash escaped Granny's rage.
Jehoiada the priest worked backstage.
    Coronation by force!
    Took out Gran like a horse!
Jo is King at just seven years of age.

24

Jo fixed up, by public subscription,
God's house; but that false-god addiction
    Fell on Jo, and he stoned
    The chap who intoned:
"God's from you!" Jo died, per prediction.

25

Amaziah was salty for war,
Slew ten thousand, dropped ten thousand more.
    He fancied their idols;
    Lost, still genocidal,
To Israel; in Lachish, was done for.

26

Uzziah's next: farmed, built and fought,
But burned incense, as only priests ought.
    To quell insurrection,
    God plagued his complexion:
Lepers had to live somewhere remote.

27

Young Jotham was next on the perch:
Nice chap, but would not go to church.
    Ammon's defeat
    Brought him silver and wheat.
That's all we know – end of research.

2 CHRONICLES

28

Incense and kids Ahaz burned.
Those Pekah took from him returned.
    He lost captives and battles
    And all temple chattels.
The God of his fathers he spurned.

29

Hezekiah was godly and true:
Told the Levites, "Jehovah wants you!"
    A four-thousand-beast scorch,
    Many songs, and clean porch
Consecrated the temple anew.

30

"Please come to our Passover bash!"
Some responded, from Zeb, Mann and Ash.
    Nineteen thousand beasts plus
    Were killed with much fuss.
Flatbread! And a grand altar-smash.

31

More idols were broken, groves cut,
And tribute proferred, quite a glut,
    What with oxen and sheep
    And grain in a heap
To feed Levites, with healthy throughput.

32

Senna besieged Hezekiah.
Hez made the dry land even drier.
    "God's bigger than them!"
    (Indeed, killed Senna's men.)
Hez grew rich, then 'twas time to expire.

33

The old tale we once more rehearse:
Mannaseh worshipped strange gods diverse;
    To Babylon took,
    His bad ways forsook.
Son Amon, quickly slain, was yet worse.

34

Josiah no false gods would brook.
His priests dug out Moses' old book.
    The King rent his clothes:
    "Now Judah God loathes!"
To obey God they all undertook.

35

Lambs and cows, forty thousand in all,
Killed for Holy Jo's Passover Ball.
    Reluctant Pharaoh
    Shot through dogged Jo:
In disguise, in his prime, came the fall.

36

Jehos three, -ahaz, -iakim and
-iachin, taken to foreign land.
    Zedekiah's no better
    And Babylon's fetters
Hold the Jews, until Persia's command.

EZRA

1

God stirred Persia's Cyrus to say,
"Israelites, be on your way!
    "Assist their reversions
    "With goods, all you Persians!
"We'll rebuild the temple today."

2

Fifty thousand, with servants; and steeds,
Seven thousand: so the comeback proceeds.
    Some who've lost track
    Of their roots still come back.
Gold's donated for rebuilding needs.

3

To Dave's city they came, to a man;
Altar built, barbecuing began.
    The new-laid foundation
    Delighted the nation:
Trumpets played, elders cheered and tears ran.

4

The foes round Jerusalem sulked.
They bothered the workers and skulked.
    They wrote Artaxerxes
    To cancel the works: he's
Obliging, to keep Persia's mulct.

5

Guv'nor Tatnai surveyed the construction:
"Who approved all this rubble and ruction?"
    "God and Cyrus! Don't harry us!"
    So Tat wrote to Darius:
"Is this true? Should we hinder production?"

6

Then King Darius rummaged, and found
By King Cyrus' decree he was bound.
    He and his helped complete.
    A new temple needs meat!
So beasts, seven hundred, were browned.

7

Artaxerxes wrote Ezra this note:
"Go and preach what your chap Moses wrote.
    "Take our silver and gold.
    "Let your God be consoled."
Ezra came, and the chief men he brought:

8

"I here list the chiefs. But we waited
"For men of Levi, consecrated.
    "At Ahava we fasted,
    "And God's favour lasted.
"Two hundred beasts burned, treasures stated."

9

"The chiefs shuffled up, and they said:
"'With Gentiles we've all interbred!'
    "I ripped clothes and hair!
    "How the Lord must despair!
"Israel cannot face God for dread!"

10

"You've sinned over-much!" Ezra cried.
Said the chaps, "Yes, but let's go inside!
    "It's too wet for divorce!
    "Let the law take its course."
In two months, they'd put strange wives aside.

NEHEMIAH

1

Nehemiah here. When I learned
Of Jerusalem's fall, its gates burned,
    I sat down and wept,
    Prayed, "Lord, please accept
"Our remorse. To your Word we've returned."

2

Artaxerxes asked, "Why do you grieve?"
Straightway offered lumber and leave.
    The walls I inspected.
    "Build 'em up!" I directed.
Gesh, San, Tobe wrongly called us naïve.

3

So now, who built up what: here's the tally
For gates named Sheep, Fish, Old and Valley,
    Dung, Fountain, Miphkad,
    Water, Horse, East, and add
Sheep, come back round, for finale!

4

Halfway through, San and Tobe and their mates
Made their minds up to knock down our gates.
    So we minded the trumpet
    And, like it or lump it,
Worked with swords to defend our estates.

5

Many groused that they'd not enough grain,
That their chiefs lent for usury's gain.
    I scolded the bosses
    To swallow their losses.
My dinner demands were humane.

6

San and Gesh wrote thus: "Come, let us meet."
I said, "Not on your Nelly! You'll cheat!"
    "Run and hide!" cried their prophet.
    I said, "Faker! Come off it!"
Built the wall, 'spite of all their deceit.

NEHEMIAH

7

I put bro' Hanani in charge:
"Guard it well, for the city is large!"
    With horses and camels
    We'd eight thousand mammals,
Fifty-K souls in our entourage.

8

On Watergate Street, Ezra read
The lawbook of Moses, and said:
    "Rejoice in God's truth!
    "Go live in a booth!"
For a week in their shelters they fed.

9

Clothed in sacks, they read out Mo's codex;
Cried, "Lord, please forgive our stiff necks!
    "You brought us from Egypt,
    "Forgave us when we slipped!
"We promise you no more to vex!"

10

Sealed anew to the Law were these folks,
To Mo's book and to all it invokes:
    The Sabbath to keep,
    The offerings to heap,
Tithes and sons to the temple's top blokes.

11

The people drew lots: one in ten
Set up home in Jerusalem; Ben
    And Jude were their dads.
    (This chapter then adds
A who's who of menfolk again.)

12

The Levites and priests here I note.
To God then these walls we devote.
    Two parties go round
    To make joyful sound.
For God's triple stores, chiefs I promote.

13

Foreign men, foreign wives, I forbid!
Tobe's stuff in the temple? Get rid!
    On the Sabbath, no lading,
    No treading, no trading!
Remember, O Lord, all I did!

ESTHER

1

Ahasuerus (that's Xerxes), the King
Of Persia, with feast in full swing,
    When his wife wouldn't come,
    Cut her off: "Girls, succumb
"To your men! All must know of this thing!"

2

So the King said, in want of a Queen,
"Gather virgins, and make sure they're clean!"
    Mordecai's cousin Esther
    Emerged from sequester:
Crown secured, and soon treason foreseen.

3

Haman's chancellor now. Mordecai
Deigns not to lower his eye.
    Ham cries, "Kill the Jews!"
    The King shrugs: "As you choose."
So the order went out from on high.

4

The Jews moaned in sackcloth and ash.
Mordecai gave his ward a tongue-lash:
    "Do your part, as I taught thee!"
    "But the King hasn't sought me!
"Still I'll go, though we'll probably clash."

5

She touched the King's gold sceptre-end,
Fed him and Haman; said, "Attend
    "Tomorrow!" But Mord
    Wouldn't bow to that lord.
Cried Ham, "Let him hang if not bend!"

6

The King recalled Mord's treason warning.
"Dress him well! Have Ham do the adorning."
    Mord paraded in style
    As Ham the Gentile
Ground his teeth, hid his head, moaned in
                                    mourning.

7

The King and Haman went to dinner.
Esther begged, "Save the Jews from this sinner!"
    "Let the gallows he built,"
    Cried the King, "bear his guilt!"
Ham's a dangling and dead discipliner.

8

The new chancellor's Mord, and he writes:
"Any Jews who are caught up in fights
    "Are licensed to kill.
    "This is at the King's will."
Persians, scared, became Israelites!

9

Came the day Ham decreed; the Jews killed.
Voices anti-Semitic they stilled:
    Eighty thousand dead men.
    They hanged Ham's sons, ten.
The feast of Purim was instilled.

10

The King taxed the cities and isles.
The details are all in the files,
    Of Mordecai's rise,
    Respected and wise,
Seeking peace throughout all of his trials.

JOB

1

Here's a pious man, humble and wealthy.
"Not surprising!" said Satan the stealthy.
    "He's blessed! Why not probe
    "The faith of this Job?"
Kin and kine killed! – But spirit still healthy.

2

"He's crying," said God, "not critiquing!"
Says Satan, "Let's try when he's creaking!"
    He afflicts Job with boils.
    Job's devout through his toils.
Three chums sit a week without speaking.

3

At last Job gives voice to dismay:
"Why born? Curse that night and that day!
    "I had rather be dead
    "Than such woes on my head!
"Fortune goes, trouble comes, come what may."

4

Eliphaz, first of chums, spoke his piece:
"You've been wise, now your burdens increase.
    "God humbles the strong.
    "Think you he can do wrong?
"Shall he trust in a mortal's caprice?"

5

"The fools meet the fate they befit.
"Man is born unto trouble. Submit
    "Your cause to the Lord.
    "Your faith he'll reward
"With good fortune, I'm certain of it."

6

"The world's sea-sand weighs less than my grief,"
Grumbled Job. "I can't get no relief!
    "You tell me, 'Don't mope!'
    "But 'tis useless to hope.
"I'm right that I'm wronged by the Chief!"

7

"Like a servant seeks shade, I need rest.
"I've no hope, I must die, I'm depressed.
    "So why not speak my mind?
    "Lord, why plague mankind?
"Why not pardon me, if I've transgressed?"

8

Bildad, next of friends, took a turn:
"Don't take on! God is just if he's stern.
    "Man's time here is short
    "And of little import.
"God will favour you, have no concern."

9

"With God," said Job, "who can contend?
"He is more than we can comprehend.
    "Neither wicked nor good
    "Have his judgement withstood.
"To argue is just a dead end."

10

"But God, do you just like to tease?
"Do you see things as we do? God, please,
    "Why do you torment
    "Those you chose to invent?
"Before I die, give me some ease!"

11

Zophar scolds him: "Job, you've got a nerve!
"God only gives what you deserve!
    "He's deep and he's wide
    "And he won't be descried.
"Be faithful, the Lord will preserve."

12

Job shrugged. "I dare say, but I too
"Understand things as well as do you.
    "Sometimes wicked folks thrive,
    "But all critters alive
"Know to God for all things credit's due."

13

"I would speak unto God, but you guys
"Talk as if you're the Lord in disguise.
    "You'd be wiser in silence.
    "God, you might do me violence,
"But say how I've sinned in your eyes."

14

"Life is short, but withal, we are judged.
"Leave us be in the time you've begrudged!
    "A tree might regrow,
    "But a dead man, not so.
"Man is gone when through life he has trudged."

15

"Wash your mouth out!" complained Eliphaz.
"You're no wiser than we are; whereas
    "Each man is unclean
    "And can't circumvene
"Darkness, pain, trouble, death, all that jazz."

16

"You lot are no help," Job declared.
"Try speaking as if you three cared!
    "God's exposed me to scorn
    "When he might have forborne.
"I've been pure, but for death I'm prepared."

17

"I'm not long for this world. As for these,
"Mockers and flatterers – please!
    "What will righteous men say?
    "Can't you all go away?
"Corruption and worms I'll appease."

18

Bildad growled: "Enough of your talk!
"Let the wicked pay heed where they walk!
    "They will dwell in the dark,
    "They will leave not a mark.
"None remember the bad when they croak."

19

"Oy gevalt!" cried Job. "Why must you vex?
"Any error of mine God corrects.
    "He took health, glory, kin,
    "Barely left me my skin.
"Him I'll see, after all these effects."

20

Said Zophar, "The wicked man's grasp
"Will hold nothing. The venom of asp
    "Will flavour his meat.
    "There is naught he can eat.
"Just a sword will the flesh of him clasp!"

21

Job snorted. "The wicked rebel
"'Gainst God's law, and they get along swell.
    "Their life's good, so why pray?
    "But they'll face wrath one day.
"We all die, 'spite the lies you guys tell."

22

Eliphaz said, "It's naught to the Lord,
"But your wickedness won't be ignored.
    "Your iniquity's strong,
    "But accept that you're wrong
"And your fortunes will soon be restored."

23

Job said, "I've a right to complain.
"I wish God would meet and explain!
    "He hides from my sight,
    "But he knows I've done right.
"Still, my fate he is free to ordain."

24

"They that depart from God's rule
"Are greedy; to the needy they're cruel.
    "They hide from the light,
    "But remain in God's sight.
"Theirs the grave, without hope of renewal."

25

Bildad said, "How wide's God's dominion!
"Do you think he respects your opinion?
    "The moon is obscure
    "In his eyes, stars impure!
"For him man's a worm – just a minion!"

26

Job barked, "Who's been helped by you chaps?
"God holds up the Earth and skycaps,
    "Makes the heavens to quake,
    "Breaks the back of the snake,
"And these signs of him are but the scraps!"

27

"My righteousness I will hold fast.
"What's the hypocrite's hope, at the last?
    "By his widows ignored;
    "Let his sons meet the sword.
"God and man spurn the wicked outcast."

28

"Fine metals are melted from stone,
"But the covert of wisdom's not known.
    "Wisdom's richer than gold,
    "Cannot be bought and sold.
"It's in God, faith and goodness alone."

29

"Oh for the days of my youth,
"When God's light was my lantern of truth!
    "I gave comfort in need,
    "Princes called for my rede.
"I was king of the world then, in sooth!"

30

"Now the children of men I disdained
"Find their pleasure in finding me pained.
    "I'm afflicted and spurned.
    "Against me God turned.
"I mourn for this fate unexplained."

31

"My righteousness I have defended.
"A book of God's case would be splendid!
    "If I've done evil deeds
    "Let the land bring forth weeds.
"Lamentations of Job are now ended."

32

Young Elihu's wrath now was kindled.
"I've listened while my patience dwindled!
    "You three are no use.
    "Your words are obtuse!
"You speak, but God's cause you have swindled!"

33

"Job, my words are for your benefit.
"While a man fades and writes his obit,
    "A messenger sent
    "Might make him repent.
"His soul is drawn back from the pit."

34

"You claim you're unfairly convicted,
"But God's just and can't be contradicted.
    "What God's done you have earned:
    "Show you've borne it and learned!
"For rebellion let Job be afflicted!"

35

"You think that God's wrong and you're right,
"Since you're blue though you've been lily-white.
    "Must God heed what you do?
    "Righteousness is for you!
"You should trust in his better eyesight!"

36

"Listen yet: God is mighty and wise.
"From the good he withdraws not his eyes.
    "He shows sinners their sins
    "So their comeback begins,
"Spreads the light on the seas and the skies."

37

"Hearken, Job, to the sound of his thunder!
"He's the guy behind all this world's wonder.
    "All things move to his voice;
    "Rain and snow at his choice.
"To question his work is your blunder."

JOB

38

"Gird thy loins, Job, and listen to me!"
Grumbled God. "Who imprisoned the sea?
    "Have you shaken the Earth?
    "Where you there at its birth?
"Who moves stars, and who sets the rain
                          free?"

39

"Did you watch the wild goat and the fawn?
"Give the ass desert lands for a lawn?
    "Make the unicorn mulish
    "Or ostriches foolish?
"Set the eagle on high crags withdrawn?"

40

"Do you mean, Job, your God to abase?"
Job blushed. "Where can I put my face?"
    "Can you do what I do?
    "See the behemoth too!
"He's rock-hard. I put him in his place!"

41

"Can you fish out leviathan, hooked?
"Shall you bind him, or serve him up cooked?
    "Flames pour from its maw!
    "Horrid teeth fill its jaw!
"By him the whole world's overlooked!"

42

Job coughed. "P'raps I spoke out of turn."
"You three fools, fourteen beasts you must
                          burn!"

    Kin and livestock Job had;
    Was a great-great-granddad.
Fortune favours the non-taciturn!

PSALMS

1

Who shuns ungodly counsel is blessed.
By God's law alone he's impressed.
    He stands like a tree;
    Sinner's chaff is blown free.
God parts righteous from those who've
                          transgressed.

2

Heathen kings think to break from God's thrall.
God laughs and then vexes them all.
    The King is in Zion!
    God says I'm his scion!
Kiss this son, or else by his wrath fall!

3

So many against me have spoken!
But God hears me, my rest is his token.
    Ten thousand don't scare me!
    Arise, God, and spare me!
The ungodly's teeth he has broken!

4

God enlarged me when I was distressed.
My godliness he will attest.
    He will set me apart.
    (Say "la!") Know your heart.
He lights me! Now I'll have a rest.

5

I nag you each morning, oh King!
You despise fools and each wicked thing!
    I will worship in fear.
    To my foes, be severe!
Let all those who trust in you sing!

6

I'm vexed, Lord, be nice, I am weak!
Save my soul or my future is bleak!
    Weeping makes my bed float
    While my enemies gloat!
Hear my prayer, Lord, and make my foes meek!

7

Oh Lord, won't you save me from those
Soul-persecutors, my foes?
    Tread me down if I've sinned,
    But let be disciplined
The wicked, who wrought their own woes.

8

I say, "Lord" is an excellent name!
At your fingers the moon and stars came.
    Beneath angels is man,
    But above, in your plan,
All the critters. How wide is your fame!

9

Lord, I praise you! Rejoice! Sing hurrah!
Thou rebukest the heathen's chutzpah!
    The wicked are doomed,
    Their works are consumed.
Remember the righteous! Say "La!"

10

Oh Lord, where on Earth are you hiding?
There are wicked men needing your chiding!
    They are godless and mean,
    They think they're not seen.
Break their arms, while the poor you are guiding.

11

If I think of my soul as a sparrow,
Then the wicked man fires the arrow!
    But sharp is God's eye;
    His wrath rains from the sky,
But spares those whose way's straight and narrow.

12

The faithful fall off and speak vanity.
Cut the lips off that utter profanity!
    God's oath is his earnest:
    Silver seared in the furnace.
Preserve, Lord, the best of humanity!

13

What gives, Lord, have I been forgotten?
I've a sorrowful heart, feeling rotten!
    Help me out, lest I die
    And delight the bad guy!
Still, mistrusting God is just not on.

14

There's no God, says the fool in his heart.
God looked and found none who were smart.
    They were filthy, they strayed.
    The poor they betrayed.
Jake will cheer at our salvation's start.

15

Who can in the temple abide?
Him who's upright, by truth fortified.
    He does no evil labour
    Nor slanders his neighbour,
No usury, nor will he slide.

16

The Lord is my God, says my soul.
Idolaters' sorrows snowball!
    My lot is okay;
    I'm advised night and day.
God preserves me from every pitfall.

17

Listen up, God! I am pure.
Hold me up, for in you I'm secure.
    Fold your wing o'er me,
    Cast the wicked down for me.
I'll wake up with you, I am sure.

18

The Lord is my shield, amen!
Blew his nose and made earthquakes again!
    With his girding of trust,
    I grind foes into dust.
Lord, save me from violent men!

19

The Lord's glory the heavens proclaim.
Like a bridegroom, the sun is aflame.
    His statutes are right,
    Purifying one's sight.
Lord, keep me from sinning and shame.

20

May Jake's God your troubles forestall;
May he listen and grant your prayers, all.
    I know what God's force is!
    Trust in him, not in horses!
We are risen, Lord, hear when we call!

21

In salvation the king's filled with joy.
You gave life and the crown to the boy!
    You'll find out God-haters
    And cook 'em like 'taters!
His enemies' heirs you'll destroy!

22

Hear me, Lord, although I'm but a worm!
I'm laughed at, and bulls make me squirm!
    You know how I mourn
    From the unicorn's horn.
Save my soul, and we'll praise you long-term!

23

My shepherd is God. Where it's green
I lie down, and I walk by the stream.
    At his side I've no fear
    In Death Valley so drear
With his bounty and mercy serene.

24

The Lord made the Earth, it is his!
Who dares go up the hill of the Wiz?
    Him God consecrates!
    Oh lift up the gates!
Who is King? That's the end of the quiz.

25

Trusted Lord, let me not be ashamed.
For my old sins I would not be blamed.
    Let your mercy and truth
    Forgive evils of youth.
Let Israel and me be reclaimed.

26

Integrity have I, and trust.
Test my heart, Lord, you'll find it robust.
    I've avoided the vain,
    I have published your name.
Cast me not with the sinners, be just.

27

I fear no one, with God on my side.
In his temple I hope I may hide.
    I will sing with head raised.
    Let his mercy be praised!
He delivers! So for him abide.

28

Speak up, lest I fall in the pit!
Draw me not to the rank hypocrite!
    Lord, render to those
    The destruction they chose!
Songs of praise for your strength I emit!

29

Ye of might, to the Lord your strength owe,
Whose voice thunders on waters below.
    It splits cedar and flame.
    Temples fill with his name.
On the flood he sits, peace to bestow.

30

Thanks, Lord, I am lifted and healed!
I was saved from the grave when I squealed.
    Though I wept, I rejoice
    That you heeded my voice.
Sackcloth gone, now your mercy's revealed!

31

Be thou, Lord, my rock and my fort.
With vain liars I would not consort.
    Let my trouble and grief
    By your mercy be brief.
Good courage, the Lord will support!

32

He is blessed who has sinned and been shriven,
Who's confessed and the Lord has forgiven.
    All godly shall pray;
    I'll teach thee the way.
Be thou wise, not a mule to be driven.

33

God is righteous, so sing his acclaim!
At his word the skies and seas came.
    No army or horse
    Or heathenish course
Shall preserve, only trust in his name.

34

The Lord I will always be blessing.
Fear God when your troubles are pressing.
    Listen, kids, speak no guile
    And he'll save you; meanwhile,
No hope for the man who's transgressing.

35

I'm bullied! Lord, stand here and fight!
I've done nothing wrong, it's just spite!
    They mocked and they gnashed!
    Lord, make them abashed!
In return you'll be praised till tonight.

36

The wicked do not fear the Lord.
For them, evil's fun, not abhorred.
    But down they'll be cast,
    For your judgement is vast.
Kindness and life's our reward.

37

The wicked get cut down, don't fret!
Let them gnash, for the Lord's your best bet!
    The meek shall inherit
    The Earth for their merit.
Trust in God and he'll see you right yet!

38

Enough with the punishments, please!
In my loins I've a loathsome disease!
    I'm feeble and broken.
    My reproofs went unspoken.
Hurry up, Lord, my sorrows appease!

39

Fearing sin, with my mouth in a bridle,
I sinned when I left my tongue idle.
    Life's short and man's vain.
    Lord, surcease from pain
I desire, before offstage I sidle.

40

The Lord brought me out of the clay.
I sing of his works every day.
    I delight in his will,
    But iniquities still
Weigh me down. Take the wicked away!

41

Be kind to the poor folk, and then
You'll be blessed. God, forgive me for when
    I have sinned. I have foes:
    Let them not round me close!
Bless God everlasting, amen.

42

I thirst for a God I can't see
While my enemies scoff, "Where is he?"
    I'm strangely depressed,
    Yet God will, I attest,
Lift my soul from the depths of the sea.

43

Plead my cause 'gainst an ungodly nation.
I'm oppressed, God, whence your abdication?
    Send your truth and your light:
    I'll sing on your site!
Chin up, soul, I've still hope in salvation!

44

God, we've heard you did well in the past;
You saved us, but now we are cast
    To the sword of the heathen,
    Forsook for no reathen!
Wake up and redeem us at last!

45

Thanks to God, you're a king full of grace.
You are righteous, your foes you efface.
    Of aloes and cassia
    And myrrh smells the gas o' ya.
Your memory time shall not erase.

46

Though the mountains by seas are assaulted,
God's our refuge. Our wars he has halted.
    He makes the Earth quiver
    From his city upriver.
"I AM GOD, AND I WILL BE EXALTED!"

47

Shout triumph for God, clap your hands!
He subdues foreign peoples and lands!
    On his heavenly chaise
    He garners our praise!
With Abraham's people he stands!

48

Now Zion's a beautiful spot.
Enter in, foreign kings, dare ye not?
    They fled from the Lord,
    For here he's adored.
Mark well how we've built on this plot.

49

Listen here, be you high, low, poor, rich:
No wealth can forestall that death, which
    Comes to wise man and brute;
    Though honour's your suit
To the grave you take nary a stitch.

50

From Zion in beauty God shined:
"If I'm hungry, I don't need mankind!
    "But offer for thanks.
    "And you wicked – your pranks?
"I'll requite them when I'm so inclined."

51

Lord, pardon transgressions profane.
With hyssop wash out my soul's stain.
    With your spirit in me
    I'll evangelise thee.
Fix Zion, we'll burn bulls again.

52

Mischievous and mighty, why boast?
With lying thy tongue is engrossed!
    God shall pluck away thee!
    Look at me, I'm a tree!
Praise God and his mercy utmost!

53

You remember what's in Psalm Fourteen?
It's all here again, and there's been
    No change, but to mention
    That bones of contention
God scattered, from fellows unclean.

54

God, judge me and save me, I pray,
For oppressors and strangers hold sway.
    But God's on my side:
    Enemies, woe betide!
From trouble God took me away.

55

I plead, 'cause my enemies sneer.
With the wings of a dove I'd get clear!
    From foes, flak is fine,
    But not you, friend of mine!
Damn my foes, God, and lend me your ear.

56

Gramercy, oh Lord, for each knave
Would follow and swallow me; they've
    Designs on my soul
    When I go for a stroll.
Turn them back, God, keep me from the grave.

57

I hide from the storm 'neath thy wings,
For 'tis God that performeth all things.
    Among lions I lie,
    Pits and traps waiting nigh!
To your glory, oh Lord, my heart sings.

58

Sons of men! Serpents! Lies are your venom!
They've wickedness built in their genome!
    Break their teeth, melt like snails,
    So their wickedness fails.
Bloodshod righteous rejoice then in plenum!

59

Bloody men! Oh Lord, save me from them!
I'm blameless, but their stratagem
    Is to harry and bark,
    But the Lord has their mark,
For their curses and lies he'll condemn.

60

God's grumpy: hard things we are shown.
"**My washpot is Moab! I've thrown**
    "**My sandal o'er Edom!**"
    Defend, Lord, our freedom:
Help us fight, we can't do it alone!

61

From the ends of the Earth I will cry.
Lead me up to rock higher than I.
    I'll hide 'neath your wing.
    You'll shelter the king.
I sing praise. May the king never die.

62

God's my rock, I shall tell you this thrice!
You're like tottering walls, men of vice!
    Degrees low and high
    Are vain and a lie.
Power's God's, I have heard it said twice.

63

Oh my God, but my flesh has a thirst!
In your praise are my lips well-rehearsed!
    Let false chatterboxes
    Be eaten by foxes!
My dreams are with thee interspersed.

64

Lord, people keep calling me names!
They shoot words with nefarious aims!
    They have secretive hearts,
    But they'll meet their own darts
When God puts an end to their games.

65

Purge my transgressions away!
Blessed is he who in your courts may stay.
    You build mountains, calm seas;
    The corn's thirst you ease.
Your gifts bring the vales a field day!

66

All ye lands, make the joyfullest noise!
God be praised in his terrible ploys
    Toward children of men.
    (Then it's Egypt again.)
For God, beasts my altar destroys.

67

Merciful God, whose face shines,
Who health to each nation assigns,
    Let us all sing in praise
    Of your bountiful ways –
Rejoice to the furthest shorelines.

68

Like smoke make your enemies flee!
Earth-shaker, we prospered with thee!
    In high hills he liveth;
    To his people he giveth;
Scatters foes; from the skies speaketh he.

69

My name's mud, and I'm stood in the mire.
So unfair, thick as hair, foes conspire.
    Give them, Lord, since you're kind,
    Loins that shake, eyesight blind!
Let's all sing, every thing, form a choir!

70

Deliver me quick, God, don't tarry!
Confound and confuse those that harry
    With their shameful 'Aha!'
    Let the rest cry 'Hurrah!'
With your love we'll be happy as Larry.

71

Lord, I trust you, my rock and my fort.
From the womb you have been my escort.
    Let me be, now I'm old,
    By salvation consoled.
I sing praise, for my foes you will thwart.

72

David's son, the next king's a good bloke:
Helps the poor, waters grass, judges folk.
    His foes shall encrust
    Him with gold, licking dust.
In blessing, his name we'll invoke.

73

I envied the rich, proud and fat,
The wicked, corrupt plutocrat;
    But I now see it all:
    They rise but to fall!
I trust God now, goodbye to all that.

74

Hey, God, you've forgotten your sheep!
Your sanctuary's burned to a heap!
    We've no prophets, just loss!
    Please show 'em who's boss!
Help your people, we need some upkeep!

75

Thanks, God! "I WILL UPRIGHTLY JUDGE.
"FOES AND FOOLS, WELL, I GAVE THEM A NUDGE."
    Not by east, north or west,
    But by God are we blessed
With God's wine; but the wicked get sludge.

76

God's in Zion, his temple in Salem.
While the stout-hearted sleep, he'll assail 'em.
    His wrath, in its violence,
    Makes the Earth stand in silence.
Fear God, for kings' crowns won't avail 'em!

77

I complained in my trouble to God:
"Where you at? Why's your service slipshod?"
>   I recalled then your wonders,
>   Your lightnings and thunders,

And the way that you led where Mo trod.

78

Tell your kids about Jacob's God's works!
After Egypt, recall we were jerks!
>   So sometimes God slew us:
>   In wrath, he saw through us.

Now for mercy in Zion he lurks.

79

Thanks to heathens, the beasts eat the saints!
Unburied, their blood the ground paints.
>   God, it must make you seethe an'
>   Pour wrath on the heathen!

Purge our sins, free us, heed our complaints!

80

Jo's shepherd, 'twixt cherubim dwelling,
Come back to us, our tears are welling!
>   Turn your bountiful shine
>   On this withering vine.

Let your countenance light this fruit swelling.

81

Form a band, and let's make joyful noise
For the feast. "Hey, I saved you tomboys!
>   "Had ye not gone a-whoring,
>   "To strange gods imploring,

"I'd have fed ye and filled ye with joys!"

82

God judges among other gods.
With justice and need they're at odds.
>   Help those of low birth!
>   Out of course is the Earth!

But they'll fall, like the princes death prods.

83

Oh God, let your silence be over,
For tumultuous foes are in clover!
>   Edom, Moab and Gebal,
>   Treat like Zeeb, Zeb and Zal:

Roll 'em off, burn 'em down, great Jehovah!

84

Thy tabernacles are amiable, Lord.
There I faint and birds nest in concord.
>   They that in thy house dwell
>   Make of Baca a well.

In thy courts and grace is my reward.

85

You favoured us, Lord, brought us back.
Soothe thy anger and keep us on track.
>   I will hear what you say:
>   Peace and goodness, your way.

With the land and the Lord we'll not lack.

86

Lord, save me to lift up my soul!
A jolly good God forgives all.
>   You're the best of the lot.
>   Though proud foes may plot,

Your comfort to me is their gall.

87

Holy mountains of Zion's foundation
Have God's love and the world's admiration.
>   He will reckon our worth
>   By the place of our birth,

Where songs spring forth in celebration.

88

Incline, Lord, your ear while I weep.
In the grave with the fallen I creep!
>   I'm half-dead and friendless!
>   Afflictions are endless.

I can't sing your praise six feet deep!

89

Lord, your faithfulness, time and again
I will praise, for you made Earth, and then
>   Gave David your favour.
>   Yet will you now waver?

Come back and play nice, Lord! Amen.

90

Thou art God, who has been and will be.
Our lives flash and fade before thee.
>   We shall wither tomorrow.
>   Match us joy for our sorrow,

So your beauty and glory we'll see.

91

You're safe in the shade of God's wing
 From snares, plagues and every bad thing.
    The Lord won't forsake,
    Though ye tread on a snake!
"He who loves me, him long life I'll bring."

92

For the Lord, it is good to sing praises.
The depth of his thoughts quite amazes!
    With him, my puny horn's
    Like a strong unicorn's!
Good men flourish; the wicked he razes.

93

God's throne lasts forever. He's dressed
In strength, and the world is at rest.
    In his might he withstood
    The voice of the flood.
Per his word, his home's endlessly blessed.

94

Don't let evil folks, Lord, win forever!
These brutes, killers, fools think they're clever.
    He who made eyes can see!
    He's a comfort to me,
For iniquity's workers he'll sever.

95

Come, let's all have a happy sing-song,
For God built the Earth, he is strong!
    We're his sheep, and he says:
    "Don't be bad, like past days.
"My wrath then was forty years long."

96

Sing a new song to big up the Lord!
He is great and he must be adored!
    He's a god, not an idol.
    Joyful trees and roars tidal
On fixed Earth await God's just reward.

97

The Earth and the isles praise God's reign.
His presence can flatten terrain.
    Graven images fail:
    It's the Lord we must hail!
In righteousness give thanks again.

98

Sing to God and his mighty right hand,
Whose salvation's all over the land.
    On harp and on horn
    Let your voices be borne!
Let the floods clap to greet his command!

99

The Lord reigns and nothing stands still.
His name's great. Jacob has his goodwill.
    Mo and Co. heard his solemn
    Conversing cloud column.
God forgave! Worship his holy hill.

100

All ye lands, make the joyfullest sound!
Raise glad voices when God is around!
    The Lord made the flock:
    We are just his livestock!
His truth's endless, his mercy unbound.

101

Wisely at home I'll behave.
Wicked things shall not my eyes deprave.
    I will cut off the proud!
    No liars allowed!
I'll destroy each deceiver and knave.

102

Incline to me, Lord, with your ears!
Like a lost bird, my life disappears.
    To our groans you won't harden
    Your heart, but grant pardon.
Our seed and you outlast the years.

103

Bless the Lord and his mercy, my soul,
Who judges, redeems, forgives all.
    If he's angry, it's meet.
    Like grass, life is fleet.
Angels and hosts, him extol.

104

Clothed in light, the Lord walks on the wind.
To the valleys and seas water's pinned.
    There are trees for the birds,
    There is grass for the herds,
Sun and moon, and an end for who's sinned.

Psalms

105
This long psalm recaps that whole script
Of Abe, Jacob, Mo and Egypt,
    How folks fled the frontiers,
    All the wilderness years,
And how land from the heathen was ripped.

106
Save me, Lord, though our fathers were sinners.
We forgot Egypt - you made us winners!
    Golden calf, Dathan burned,
    Heathen idols - we've turned
More times than we've made you hot dinners!

107
The good Lord gathered us from the wild.
Chained rebels felt his mercy mild.
    The afflicted he saves;
    He calms the sea's waves.
With water and food the land's piled.

108
Up early to sing the Lord's praise!
He's glorious, holy! He says:
    "SHECHEM, SUCCOTH AND EDOM:
    "I'LL TAKE 'EM - YOU NEED 'EM!"
Lead us on, God, the city to raze!

109
The wicked who lie, to my hurt,
Let his curses become his hair-shirt!
    May his children and wife
    Inherit his strife!
But for me, Lord, your mercy exert.

110
"SIT DOWN HERE! REST THY FEET ON THE STOOL
"OF THINE ENEMIES' HEADS 'NEATH YOUR RULE.
    "THESE LANDS WE WILL FILL
    "WITH THE HEATHENS WE KILL.
"LIFT YOUR HEAD AS YE DRINK FROM THE POOL."

111
In assembly, praise God, oh my heart.
His wonders are all works of art!
    Gave us lands in his charity
    With judgement and verity.
Fear of God's commands, that's wisdom's start.

112
That man's blessed who is God-fearing, which is
Why righteousness brings wealth and riches.
    Heart fixed on God's light,
    He works for what's right.
In fury the wicked man twitches.

113
Offer up praise to God's name!
All day long he compels our acclaim.
    He lifts poor from the dung
    To the top social rung!
He gives babes to the infertile dame!

114
When Israel escaped Egypt's cordon,
The sea fled and so did the Jordan.
    Like sheep were the mountains,
    The rocks weak as fountains,
All a-tremble before Jacob's warden.

115
Give glory to God, for he's real!
The idols of heathens don't feel.
    They're dead as the dust.
    In God we must trust.
Bless the Lord, for he's blessed us with weal.

116
When compassed by trouble and sorrow
I besought God a better tomorrow.
    He lent me relief.
    I affirm my belief
And pay thanks for the fortune I borrow.

117
All nations, praise God for his mercies!
That's all that this short song rehearses.
    It would not avail
    To add more detail:
There's none, for there's only two verses!

118
All proclaim that God's mercy endures.
The fate of my foes he ensures
    With his valiant right hand.
    'Neath his gates I will stand.
Our prosperity his light secures.

119

Let your righteous laws, Lord, me enlighten.
Quash the proud, but not those your words
                                   frighten.
    Your laws are so sweet!
    I love them! (Repeat
All this grovelling *ad infinitum*.)

120

Lord, deliver me, lest I fall for
Deceivers and liars galore!
    Give 'em juniper coals!
    Around Kedar's tent-poles
I'm for peace, but the rest are for war.

121

See the hills, whence God sends me his aid.
He won't sleep. Earth and heaven he made.
    The sun shan't thee smite,
    Nor the moon in the night.
Go thou in or out, God is thy shade.

122

Oh goody, we're off to God's place!
The big city in whose small space
    Our thanks we express.
    By the thrones God will bless
With goodness and peace all our race.

123

To heaven and God my eyes roll,
As the low gaze on those in control.
    Have mercy! We're cowed
    By the easy and proud:
Their scorn and contempt fill my soul.

124

Had the Lord never held us in worth,
There would be an Israelite dearth.
    We'd be lost 'neath the flood
    If it weren't for the good
Of our God, who made heaven and earth.

125

Like Zion, God's faithful shan't cease;
He surrounds us, prevents our decrease.
    Let no wicked rod
    Blight the people of God.
Judge the crooked, give Israel peace.

126

From bondage the good Lord retrieves
His people; and who disbelieves
    Sees now God is great:
    As streams turn their spate,
Who weeps as he sows laughs with sheaves.

127

Not the guard, but the Lord, will deliver
The city; of sleep, he's the giver.
    As fruit on the barrow,
    As a mighty man's arrow
Are children: let each fill his quiver.

128

Who fears God and gives his ways attendance,
Is blessed with the fruit of dependants.
    Happy man! For thou should
    See Jerusalem's good,
Peace in Israel, many descendants.

129

Afflicted from youth! But somehow,
Though they furrowed my back with their plough,
    The Lord loosed our cords
    And like withered greenswards
On a roof are our enemies now.

130

Out of the depths I have cried.
Who can stand when God's not on their side?
    I wait, as for dawn,
    And when God's wrath's withdrawn
Let his bounteous mercy abide.

131

High things my eyes aren't toward.
I have cut my umbilical cord.
    My heart is not haughty,
    I've never been naughty.
Henceforth let us hope in the Lord.

132

Dave here! And I won't bed down
Till I've found you some digs in the town.
    You said, "KEEP MY LAWS
    "AND THIS KINGDOM IS YAWS!
"YOUR KIDS FLOURISH, SO DOES YOUR CROWN."

133

How sweet to be all coalescing!
Like the whiskers of Aaron when messing
    With dribbles of ointment,
    Or that dewy appointment
When the good Lord commanded the blessing.

134

Temple servants who pull graveyard shift,
Let your lips bless the Lord, your arms lift!
    He made heaven, you know,
    And earth down below.
(To add more is not in my gift.)

135

We're the good Lord's peculiar treasure.
All things made and done at his pleasure:
    Pharaoh's fate! Wind and rain!
    Idolatry's vain!
Give him blessings and praise at your leisure!

136

Thank God! He makes wonders, he's clever,
Stood by us through every endeavour.
    Slew famous kings!
    Our heritage brings!
For his mercy endureth for ever.

137

By the rivers of Babylon, yea,
We wept when commanded to play,
    Remembering Zion.
    When Edom's babes die on
The stones, we'll be happy that day.

138

Before all the gods, thee I'll praise.
You strengthened me in my malaise.
    When they hear ye, each king
    Shall of your glory sing.
Don't forsake those you worked out of clays.

139

Up and down, in and out, I am known,
Where I've fled or I've lain or I've flown,
    By the Lord, day and night;
    He surpasses me quite.
No wickedness will I condone.

140

Mischief and evil and snakes!
The wicked man traps for me makes!
    Oh Lord, take them down!
    Let them win no renown.
The righteous maintain, for our sakes.

141

Oh Lord, on my lips your constraint is
A must, lest I eat wicked dainties!
    Let the righteous throw stones.
    Each man's grave takes his bones.
I trust God, keep me clear of what ain't his.

142

To the Lord I have cried supplication:
I'm beset with their snares and predation.
    None but I knew my hand.
    Hear me, Lord! In the land
Of the living you're my preservation.

143

God, listen, don't judge, for the foe
Has smitten my life, brought me low.
    For your kindness I thirst.
    Destroy all the worst,
But to me your deliverance show.

144

The Lord is the strength of my arms.
His titanic power alarms!
    Free me from that reviled
    Strange false-handed child.
Thanks to God, fruitful families and farms.

145

Thy great works I've praised, man and boy.
All will thy goodness enjoy.
    Thy kingdom's eternal,
    Thy kind care paternal,
But all wicked men you will destroy.

146

Praise the Lord, don't trust princeling nor man,
Whose thoughts die at the end of their span.
    Our God is our hope,
    He helps us all cope,
But the wicked he sends down the pan.

Psalms

147

God gathers and binds, names each star,
Feeds ravens, makes strong the gate's bar,
    Casts down wicked dregs,
    Dislikes horses and legs,
Favours no other nation (so far).

148

Heavens and hosts, praise the Lord.
By sun, moon and stars he's adored.
    They'll all last forever.
    Men humble and clever
Praise his name, for Israel is his ward.

149

Let Israel in their Lord rejoice!
Play the timbrel, all dance, lift your voice!
    For our folk please the Lord.
    Saints sing with a sword,
For judging the heathen's their choice.

150

Praise God in the firmament's rays!
Praise the Lord for his mighty displays!
    Praise him with timbrels,
    With trumpets and cymbals!
Let all things that breathe offer praise.

PROVERBS

1

The proverbs of Sol are acute.
Pay attention, 'cos wisdom's a hoot.
    Have no truck with thieves!
    Wisdom cries, "Who believes
"Shall be safe! The rest eat their own fruit."

2

Let Solomon be your professor
That strange woman? Don't try to impress 'er!
    She'll corrupt - don't succumb!
    Instead, strive to become
Upright man, not uprooted transgressor.

3

Let the Lord and his laws your heart claim.
Take your lumps, wisdom's riches attain,
    Tree of life and of knowledge!
    Take his works for your college.
The wise shall have glory, fools shame.

4

Listen up, for your father is talking,
Wisdom's crown of grace ever evoking.
    Cleave to all that you learn,
    And the wicked man - spurn!
Eyes front, lad, and watch where you're walking!

5

Honeyed lips, oily mouth? Her end's bitter!
The wisdom you're offered, don't fritter!
    Cisterns, wells, rivers:
    Instruction delivers!
Your wife's bosom friend be - not a titter!

6

Consider the ways of the ant!
A naughty man's feet utter cant!
    There are six things, or seven,
    Offensive to heaven.
Pretty whores are a snare to enchant.

7

Let wisdom thy wanderlust quell,
Lest ye join some loose maid's clientèle.
    Your qualms she dismisses
    With perfumes and kisses,
But her chamber's the gateway to hell!

8

Wisdom cries out from the heights:
"More than gold, understanding delights.
    "Great men heed my word!
    "Creation I spurred!
"Who hears me God's favour invites."

9

'Twixt seven poles wisdom is spread.
Treat with wise men, not scorners instead.
    Cries the fool on her seat,
    "Stolen water is sweet!"
But ye'll break secret bread with the dead.

PROVERBS

10
The wise understand things, Sol says,
While the prating fool wastes words and days.
    The righteous he'll cherish;
    The wicked shall perish.
(All this rehearsed thirty-two ways.)

11
Being wise will the righteous assist.
The wicked man's lost and not missed.
    An indiscreet maiden
    Is a sow's nose gold-laden.
Bad things bad, good things good, that's the gist.

12
Words from the wicked, don't trust.
No evil befalleth the just.
    Till and harvest your field,
    Wisdom's fruit will it yield.
The righteous don't die, as fools must.

13
Shut your mouth for a fat fruity soul.
The rich and the poor shall swap role.
    Unearned wealth will diminish;
    Good's repaid at the finish.
Love your son, chasten him with a pole.

14
She is foolish who plucks down her dwelling.
For foul oxen the case is compelling.
    What seems right may bring death.
    Labour well, don't waste breath.
Acclaim nations in wisdom excelling.

15
Tree of life, yea, the wholesome tongue's that.
Lack of merriment sorrows begat.
    God's far from the sinner!
    Not stalled ox, herb dinner!
A good report makes the bones fat.

16
You may think you're clean, but God knows.
Where he directs, that's where man goes.
    Beware wrath of kings!
    Life's in wisdom's wellsprings.
The Lord will your cast lot dispose.

17
God fines hearts as men silver and gold.
Grandkids are the crown of the old.
    Choose bereft bears o'er folly.
    Does you good to be jolly!
Fools seem wise when their tongues are on hold.

18
Fools' words are a snare to engross.
Wealth's a fort of conceit, grandiose.
    Speak too soon, ye do wrong.
    Death and life on the tongue.
It's good to have friends and wives close.

19
Better poor than perverse. Fast feet sin.
Wealth makes friends, liars die, and akin
    To dew is king's favour.
    Wise counsel's thy saver.
Smite who scorns, and let fools be whipped in.

20
Drink makes drunks, don't vex kings, for their eyes
Banish evil. Hearts' deep water's wise.
    God hates measures phoney.
    False bread's sweet but stony.
A blue wound belly-cleansing supplies.

21
God steers a king's heart through his life.
Small cell beats big house with loud wife.
    No riches in wine!
    Keep loose lips in line!
Horse for battle, but God saves from strife.

22
Name and favour beat valuable things.
Wealth and honour the fear of God brings.
    Sloth avoids the big cat!
    All beware strange girls' chat!
He who's diligent stands before kings.

23
Don't covet the false meats of kings.
Beat thy son, let thy lips speak right things.
    A whore's a deep ditch.
    Don't let red wine bewitch:
It unmans thee and like a snake stings.

PROVERBS

24
Let wisdom thy chambers adorn.
Fools sin, and it's loathsome to scorn.
    Wisdom's rich, honey-sweet.
    Don't laud foes' defeat.
The sloth's vineyard bears nettle and thorn.

25
Unsearchable kings search God's wonder.
Frowardness before kings is a blunder.
    Good words are golden.
    Fed foes are beholden.
Lawless souls are towns fallen to plunder.

26
Don't indulge, swing the rod! For the prater,
Like a dog to its sick, comes back later.
    Deplore the talebearer -
    Less strife where he's rarer!
Each pit traps its own excavator.

27
None can count on tomorrow, alas!
Secret love plain rebuke will surpass.
    Like rain, maid's objections!
    Hearts meet in reflections.
You'll have milk of goats, herbs, lambs and grass.

28
Knaves are pussies; each saint's a big cat.
Hear the law, or God won't hear your chat.
    A bad ruler's a bear.
    Nouveau riche, now beware!
Put your trust in the Lord and get fat.

29
Stiffnecked 'spite reproof, he's done for.
The unwise spends his self on the whore.
    The fool utters all.
    On thy son let blows fall.
Just, unjust, each the other abhor.

30
To the word of God add not one thing!
Pray thee, Lord, neither want nor wealth bring.
    Some have sword-teeth galore!
    Lists of three now – no, four.
Go well, lion, goat, greyhound, king!

31
Kings' wisdom, men's woes, wine negates.
Speak justly for wretches in straits.
    Good women are rare:
    She gives all, takes care;
Let her works be her praise in the gates.

ECCLESIASTES

1
I'm the Preacher, Dave's son. All is vanity,
For the wind and sea outlast humanity.
    Since this old world's begun
    Nothing's new 'neath the sun.
In wisdom's much grief and insanity.

2
No use chasing pleasure and mirth.
In vain accrue wealth from the earth.
    Sage and fool die the same:
    None remembers thy name.
To the saints sinners pass all their worth.

3
Every thing in its season: to die,
To plant, pluck and kill, laugh and cry.
    There's no profit can last.
    God requires what is past.
Rejoice in one's work, for death's nigh.

4
Better be dead than oppressed.
The fool will his own flesh ingest.
    When all's said and done,
    Two are better than one.
Folks live and die: I'm unimpressed.

5
Do not babble and play the fool's part.
Silver greed won't for silver depart.
    Hoarding riches is vain:
    We die wretched again.
God's answer is joy in one's heart.

ECCLESIASTES

6

God makes a man rich, not content.
What you reap can't make hunger relent.
   Live two millennia,
   Gather wisdom, sire many a
Son, your life's still shadows spent.

7

One grows wise in one's heart when one mourns.
Fools' laughter's the crackling of thorns.
   One man, no maid, in a
   Thousand's no sinner.
Though made upright, his nature man scorns.

8

Wise men shine. By the king's law be bound.
Time and judgement your purpose confound.
   Men suffer injustice.
   Favour mirth, for my thrust is
God's works on Earth cannot be found.

9

A living dog beats a dead cat.
Work, wine, wife: take your joy in all that.
   Battle's not to the strong.
   Naught can thy life prolong.
One sinner the wise can't combat.

10

It stinks when with folly wise dabble.
Set not princes and rich 'mongst the rabble.
   Snakes bite from the hedge.
   Give your woodaxe an edge.
Houses fall, money talks and fools babble.

11

Spread your bread. A tree lies where it falls.
You must tend crops howe'er the wind calls.
   Unborn bones God perceives -
   You just gather your sheaves.
Enjoy youth, but know God judges souls.

12

In good times remember the Lord;
Don't wait for the dark days abhorred.
   There are too many books!
   Here's how wisdom looks:
Fear God: by your works you'll be scored.

SONG OF SOLOMON

1

Kisses better than wine, he smells good!
Upright love has the king, he's a stud!
   I'm comely and black.
   He'll rest on my rack.
Our bed's green, and we don't lack for wood!

2

Call me Rose, Sharon, thorn-circled Lil'.
My fruity love sleeps, makes me ill.
   In spring, we who flirt'll
   Give ear to the turtle.
My love, turn, like a hart on a hill.

3

He's gone from my bed and the city!
Now he's back from the wilds! A committee
   Of swords guard his sheets.
   Chariot in the streets,
With his ma's crown King Sol ain't half pretty!

4

Scarlet lips, teeth of sheep, eyes of dove,
Fruity temples, goat hair up above!
   With cinnamon smell,
   Myrrh and aloes as well!
Taste my spices and garden fruits, love!

5

Wet feet and hair, where are the towels?
My love's hand in the hole moved my bowels.
   He's gone, left me thus!
   Girls ask why all the fuss,
But his beauty outshines all their growls.

6

In the garden he takes his delight!
His hair's goatish, his teeth woolly-white!
   - She's prettier than most,
   Like an invading host!
Return like twin troops, Shulamite!

7

Your foot's at its best in a boot,
But golly, the rest of you's cute!
    You're like clusters of vine!
    - Let's check out that wine!
Try the grapes! Mandrakes smell! Have some fruit!

8

My bro sucked mom's breasts! Sup my juice!
'Neath the apple tree you were let loose.
    My sister's flat-chested,
    But I'm tower-breasted!
On these mountains of spice, be my moose!

ISAIAH

1

"ISRAEL, YOU'RE REVOLTING AND SICK!
"YOUR OFFERINGS ARE TAKING THE MICK.
    "I'LL WASH RED SINS WHITE
    "IF YOU'LL LEARN TO DO RIGHT,
"FADING OAKS, ELSE YOU'LL BURN LIKE A STICK!"

2

God will judge from his house on the peak.
Common idols and wealth great men seek.
    High things he'll bring low:
    To the bats idols go,
And to clefts in the rock you will sneak!

3

The Lord removes all but the dirt
From our land, and to each his desert.
    For the people, no king;
    For the women, no bling.
Men fall, and maids weep for their hurt.

4

Seven maids beg for one man's good name.
The fruit of the earth exiles claim.
    They of Zion are holy,
    Where homes, high or lowly,
Bear God's glory, in cloud and in flame.

5

Though the vineyard's well kept, we're wild grapes,
So to exile the Lord makes us traipse.
    Hell's mouth opens wide
    For who casts God aside.
He'll send enemies - no one escapes.

6

Fed coal by six-winged seraphim,
I saw God on his throne, heard their hymn.
    "GO CHIDE FOLKS, HOT LIPS,
    "FOR THEIR DEAF AND BLIND SLIPS!
"I'LL LAY WASTE, BUT THINGS AREN'T WHOLLY
                        GRIM."

7

Ahaz was assailed by two kings,
But God said not to fret about things:
    When the butter-boy's wise,
    They'll be pestered by flies.
In the vineyard the thorny briar clings.

8

Mahershalalhashbaz, of him write;
To the prophetess born. God will smite
    Assyrian kings,
    But the stumble-stone brings
Wizards, hunger, snares, curses and night.

9

Still some light, limits on joy and harm.
Adversaries combine and alarm.
    A prince of peace born,
    We yet face God's scorn.
Faithless folly, and each eats his arm.

10

Woe to the wicked! God's champ,
Assyria's king, will revamp
    Israel fallen,
    Though all like him swollen
Shall be hewn, and their armies decamp.

11

Jesse's line brings one wise with strong speech.
Babies play with their asp-holes, and each
    Beast lies with its prey.
    Those driven away
Now return, and the Red Sea's a beach.

ISAIAH

12

Praise God, when we're no longer spurned,
From whom for salvation you've yearned.
    Drink joy from his well.
    May our songs his fame swell!
Cry and shout, for the Lord God's returned.

13

In fury God summons a horde
To put Babylon to the sword.
    With darkness and anguish
    The dead land shall languish,
Children torn, women raped, pride's reward.

14

They're our slaves when the Lord breaks their rod.
Covet heaven? Thy carcass is trod!
    Thy people's dissolved!
    The Lord is resolved!
Snakes regrow, still more woe: trust in God.

15

In Moab they go without hair.
It's silence or weeping round there.
    Even soldiers cry now.
    A three-year-old cow!
Also drought, blood and howling despair.

16

Lost nestlings cast out, Moab's maids,
But the mercy of Dave's throne pervades.
    Though all Moab howls
    With harps in their bowels,
Their prayers and wines fail, their land fades.

17

Sheepish Damascus is shorn,
Its land but the last ears of corn.
    Forgetting salvation,
    They reap desolation.
Rushing nations are gone by the morn.

18

Woe to they who, beyond Ethiopia,
Think us lost, for God pre-cornucopia
    With the harvest communes,
    Feeds the fowl as he prunes,
Gathers us to his Zion utopia.

19

And God has it in for Egyptians.
Without water or fish, they've conniptions.
    They of realpolitik
    Slide like drunkards in sick.
Smiting, saving, they're both God's prescriptions.

20

"GO NAKED, ISAIAH!" cried God.
('Twas when Tartan took over Ashdod.)
    Thus Egypt is shown
    How she'll be overthrown,
By three years of some old prophet's bod.

21

Grievous vision and terrible wind!
The watchman saw chariots: twinned
    Horsemen, some camels,
    Asses, lions; these mammals
Proved Babylon lost, Kedar thinned.

22

Thou art a tumultuous town!
For Jerusalem's fall, prophet's frown.
    Baldness and mourning!
    Accountant, take warning!
Whom the Lord shall nail up he'll cut down.

23

Zidon trades with Tarshish no more.
Laid waste and still is that shore;
    Forgotten frontiers,
    But in seventy years
That land serves God's folks like a whore.

24

All is shattered, the earth is undone!
Men are scattered, their mirth is all gone!
    Cities fallen, prayers risen,
    But our kings are in prison,
Moon-confounding and shaming the sun.

25

God who's razed strangers' towns, thee I trust
To guard from sun's heat and storm's gust.
    For us all, a fat feast!
    And Moab is deceased!
He brings down the high fort into dust.

26

In Judah's God's righteous domain.
Lofty cities he crushed with disdain.
    Our old lords are dead;
    He's our keeper instead.
Earth discloses her blood and her slain.

27

Crooked serpents and dragons God slays.
Jacob's folk flourish in latter days.
    We are purged by this token:
    When idols are broken;
Gathered home when the great trumpet plays.

28

Priest, prophet, Ephraim, all sloshed,
Judgement stumbling, their tables unwashed!
    Their treaty with hell
    Will not serve them well.
Plowman's cummin and fitches aren't squashed.

29

Woe to Ariel, seiged and afflicted!
Yet like dreams shall thy foes be evicted.
    To wisdom made blind,
    Jake's folks one day find
Their shame gone and their faults contradicted.

30

To trust in the Pharaoh is shaming:
False idols, false prophets proclaiming.
    Like pots God will break us,
    But will not forsake us.
His breath's deluge, and brimstone inflaming.

31

Trust in God, not in Egypt's strong horses,
For the Lord will come down on their forces
    Like a bird and a lion
    Defending Mount Zion
Till Assyrians turn in their courses!

32

Righteous kings, but the churls still harass.
Go nude but for sackcloth, each lass!
    Forts and cities shall crumble,
    But God grows, for our grumble,
Blessèd land where we send forth the ass!

33

Let treacherous spoilers be spoiled.
All nations but Zion are foiled.
    With flames the Lord scours!
    Who has counted the towers?
Like a river around us God's coiled.

34

Heaven rolls up and the Lord
Burns the world with his fat bloody sword!
    Idumea's a haven
    For bittern and raven.
It's the dragons' and unicorns' sward.

35

The desert shall bring forth the rose.
Where dragons lay, now the stream flows.
    Witness God's recompense.
    Here's a holy road, whence
No sinner nor raging beast goes.

36

Assyrian Rab came, implored:
"Why trust in a Pharaoh or Lord?
    "Your God drives our forces!
    "Have two thousand horses!
"You can't beat us!" But he was ignored.

37

Isaiah told Hez what he knew:
"Don't worry, Assyria's through."
    "All gods fall!" blustered Rab.
    God dismissed their land-grab:
One-eighty-five thousand he slew.

38

Sick Hez reached the end of life's toil.
God relented o'er his mortal coil.
    "I'll sing now!" Hez cried.
    "I thought to have died,
"But Isaiah slapped figs on my boil!"

39

King Hez displayed every knick-knack
To Babylon's King Merodach.
    Cried Iz, "In that land
    "Shall your sons be unmanned!"
Hez shrugged and said, "I'm all right, Jack!"

40
Flesh is grass! Crooked land he has levelled.
In his pardon and care we have revelled.
    None can God encompass!
    No idols can trump us!
By fatigue, through God, we're not bedevilled.

41
"I gave thee a conquering king.
"I chose thee and to thee I cling.
    "Where the wild land is worst
    "I grow trees, answer thirst.
"Others vain, they are not worth a thing."

42
"In judgement my servant won't shout.
"Blind men see! Those imprisoned come out!"
    Let all for God sing!
    Destruction he'll bring!
Feel his rage for our deafness and doubt!

43
"I'll keep thee from drowning and burning.
"From the ends of the earth you're returning!
    "I am God, only me!
    "I crush armies, part sea!
"Give me beef fat, not sin! It's concerning."

44
"My spirit I'll pour on thy seed.
"I am God! They're mistaken indeed
    "Who make idols graven,
    "Their creed crass and craven.
"I built Zion! None can me exceed!"

45
"Cyrus, Jake's people, none dares
"Stand against thee! With me none compares!
    "Other lands fall to thee,
    "For they prayed to a tree!
"To God all knees bow, each tongue swears."

46
"The idols of Nebo and Bel
"Were so heavy, they and their beasts fell,
    "But, stronger than gold,
    "I bear you till you're old
"With salvation in Zion as well."

47
"Virgin of Babylon, come!
"Go naked, grind wheat and sit dumb!
    "I gave you Jake's folk:
    "You laid on the yoke!
"A widow bereft you've become!"

48
"Iron-necked, ye will not heed my signs!
"Notwithstanding, my anger declines.
    "The world's made by my hand.
    "Hearken to my command!
"Going home, thy God water-divines!"

49
I'm God's sword, we're his chosen elite.
He'll make prisoners free and replete.
    Zion is not forsaken:
    It and Gentiles awaken,
While oppressors their own flesh shall eat.

50
"Have I sold you to pay what I borrow?
"I dry seas, darken heaven!" Each morrow
    He wakes me to hear.
    Flint-faced, I've no fear.
Trust your own light, ye'll lie down in sorrow.

51
"Zion blooms for your patriarch's God!
"Though you've trembled beneath thy Lord's rod,
    "Thy sorrows assuage:
    "The cup of my rage
"Shall quench those who on my people trod."

52
Now Zion's clean, free and awake!
God brings back those Assyrians take.
    Good tidings ye'll sing!
    Bear forth each sacred thing!
At the sight of his servant kings quake.

53
This servant, the arm of the Lord,
Grows up ugly, despised and ignored,
    Yet his dumb intercession
    Repairs our transgression
And his own reputation's restored.

54

Barren woman, break forth into song!
In the big tent your people prolong!
    The Lord is your spouse!
    He'll bling up your house!
They'll not prosper who purpose you wrong.

55

Free drinks! Sure as David commands,
Other nations shall run to these lands.
    God's thoughts grow the garden.
    The wicked he'll pardon.
Mountains sing and the trees clap their hands!

56

The strangers feel strange, eunuchs dry,
But if faithful, they're good in God's eye.
    Have a name, not a son!
    Let the strangers have fun!
Blind watchmen? Let sleeping dogs lie.

57

"Adulterer, sorceress, whore:
"False idols your false sons adore,
    "But me they don't fear.
    "The contrite I keep near;
"For the wicked, no peace, evermore."

58

"You disport and dispute in your fast!
"It's for kindness, to feed the outcast!
    "If ye loosen the yoke
    "On the wretchedest folk
"Ye'll be blessed, heard, restoring the past."

59

Though God's patient attention won't cease,
Your plot's hatched like a vile cockatrice.
    What are we, in sin's snares?
    Mourning doves, roaring bears!
Keep God's word, though he dons judgement's fleece.

60

In darkness, God's light will enfold.
Other nations bring camels and gold.
    Let the world see you're blessed!
    Thou shalt suck the king's breast!
Sun and moon fade before God, behold!

61

I preach God's good news to the meek.
Of his vengeance and nurture I speak.
    When Zion's rebuilt
    We're repaid to the hilt,
And he clothes me in salvation chic.

62

Zion shines, a new name it has taken:
Hephzibah, Beulah, awaken!
    Bride to God and your sons
    Ye shall eat your own buns!
For thy city's sought out, not forsaken.

63

From Edom in fury, wine-treader!
We're the grapes of your wrath, there's none redder!
    No more do us violence,
    Your bowels in silence!
Of blessings be once more our spreader!

64

Spread your fame with your flame-flowing tricks!
For God knows what man barely predicts.
    We've made stains in our blotter:
    Remould us, great potter!
Burnt Zion's a waste! Come and fix!

65

"There's bad broth and rebellion in Zion!
"I will punish each father and scion!
    "But good times I'll save
    "For the ones who behave.
"Dust for serpents, but straw for the lion."

66

"You whose offerings look like dogs' dinners!
"The poor and contrite are the winners
    "In my new world to come
    "Where all will succumb
"And we'll gaze on worm-ridden dead sinners!"

JEREMIAH

1

Jerry here! I told God, "Come off it!
"I'm a kid, how can I be a prophet?"
    God said, "I'll defend thee,
    "Though none shall befriend thee.
"Let Jerusalem fend its foes off it!"

2

"I'm a spring, your false gods broken baths!
"Like camel, ass, harlot, wild paths
    "You have chosen o'er me.
    "Well, just wait and see.
"You think you've not sinned? Do the maths!"

3

"Whore-browed, ye have strayed, hence this drought!
"Judah saw what Israel was about,
    "Yet they too played bawd.
    "Still, you're my wife, though flawed,
"So return!" Lord, we've not been devout!

4

"Mend your ways, turn to me, circumcise!
"Flee to forts, gird your loins, cry your cries!
    "Dry winds rise, kings' hearts shrink!
    "I'll scourge earth to the brink
"With murderers, anguish, black skies!"

5

"Though punished, your ways you won't mend.
"To harlots and strange gods you bend!
    "You will suffer the yoke!
    "You think this is a joke?
"False prophets too?! Where will it end?"

6

"By night siege and war, be corrected!
"Husband, wife, young and old, all affected!
    "Ye would not walk my ways!
    "Northmen bring you cruel days!
"You're false metal the Lord has rejected."

7

"In the gates of my house, give critiques:
"False gods you've fed, up Tophet's peaks.
    "Tell Jerusalem, Jerry!
    "Where they kill, there they'll bury!
"In the desolate city none speaks!"

8

"Faithless bones 'neath the sun, as at slaughter,
"Spread like dung, and let gall be your water.
    "Be with serpents entwined!
    "Pine for peace! Ye'll not find
"In Gilead balm for my daughter."

9

I weep, but cannot get apart
From traitors. Trust none if you're smart.
    "Your deceits make me seethe an'
    "Cast you 'mongst the heathen,
"For you're uncircumcised in the heart!"

10

Gilded trees crafted by crafty men
Do no harm and no good. Way back when,
    'Twas our God made the world
    As the heavens unfurled.
Judah now is for dragons a den.

11

Ye have done what Mo's tablet forbids!
Pray to strange gods, end up on the skids!
    Anathoth's threatening me!
    "Oh, they would? Well, let's see:
"Death by sword and starvation for kids."

12

Judge the wicked, Lord, don't let them thrive!
"You're forsaken! Those rogues who connive
    "To lay waste the land,
    "Feel the back of my hand!
"Ye'll return, and your land ye'll revive."

13

"Like a clean girdle's stained in a pit,
"So on this evil people I spit!
    "Like wine jugs, you're smashed!
    "In darkness abashed,
"Carried off, for ye scorned holy writ!"

14

No water, gates, rain, crop or grass!
For our sins, thirsty kids, hungry ass!
    "Their works I examine!
    "False prophets find famine!
"My sword slays!" May this punishment pass!

15

"By swords, dogs, birds, beasts you'll be rent!
"This not Moses and Sam could prevent!"
    But I have been prayerful!
    "You'll be fine if you're careful.
"Treasures gone, to your enemies sent!"

16

"Young and old drop like dung - and no grieving!
"Serves 'em right for in strange gods believing!
    "To the north ye'll be scattered,
    "But lest all faith is shattered,
"Ye'll return to the land you're now leaving."

17

"Writ in stone, Judah's sins are entrenched.
"Like a riverbank tree you'll be drenched
    "If in me ye will trust.
    "Keep the sabbath - you must!
"Or in Zion fires will not be quenched."

18

"As a bad pot remoulded revives,
"So 'tis me decides which nation thrives.
    "Let them mend their affairs!"
    But they hunt me with snares!
Don't forgive, make 'em pay with their lives!

19

"This city I'll smash (tell them, prophet!)
"Like a bottle! Say slaughter, not Tophet!
    "Folks will hiss at this town!
    "Gobble all your kids down!
"Still ye burn to false idols! Leave off it!"

20

Pashur heard and put Jerry in stocks!
"Die in Babylon, Pash - them's the knocks!
    "Oh, but Lord, I am scorned!
    "Evildoers, be warned!
"Curse my birth, for my road is all rocks!"

21

King Zed said, "We need a good turn!"
Said Jerry, "Forget it! You'll learn!
    "God's on Babylon's side!
    "Sword and famine abide!
"He's agin' you, this city will burn!"

22

"Now go tell them this, Jeremiah:
"I've no use for the sons of Josiah.
    "Ye who worshipped astray
    "Shall, um, die, far away!
"No king grows from the seed of Coniah."

23

"False shepherds mislead in my name!
"Baal, Samaria - prophets to blame!
    "Your own dreams you've enshrined -
    "You must think I am blind!
"You're forgot! Begone, burdened by shame."

24

There were figs good and bad in a basket!
It's a vision! Now hear God unmask it.
    "The good ones I'll banish,
    "The bad I'll make vanish
"By sword, famine and pox, to their casket!"

25

For twenty-three years I've been saying
That for three-score and ten you'll be staying
    In Babylon's hands.
    Across all the world's lands
God's furious sword sweeps a-slaying.

Jeremiah

26
Jerry said, "God'll raze ya to rubble!"
"Take it back!" cried the king. "No, this snub'll
    "Remain, can't oblige ya!"
    "Hear, hear!" cried Urijah.
The king ran him through for his trouble.

27
"Send yokes and these words to all nations:
"Bend to Babylon! No protestations!
    "Else it's sword, famine, pox!
    "Can ye save temple stocks,
"Lying prophets, with vain proclamations?"

28
Han said, "Babylon's rule is now broke!"
Jerry snorted: "I wish! But their yoke
    "Is of iron, not wood.
    "Since you're up to no good,
"You shall perish." And Han did soon croak.

29
"Dear exiles, Please keep multiplying.
"With my law be ye always complying.
    "Yours, God, p.p. Jerry."
    Meanwhile Shem tried to bury
The prophet. He'll pay for defying.

30
"There'll be peace - write this down in a tome.
"After bondage I'll bring you all home.
    "Ye shall be chastised,
    "But no longer despised.
"Through the world will my wild whirlwind
                          roam!"

31
"Your captivity, that was a warner!
"Each come home and be no more a mourner.
    "In the new dispensation
    "I'll forgive deviation.
"Rebuild, Hananeel to horse corner!"

32
"Bad prophecy!" King Zed complained.
"The field of my cousin, obtained
    "By right means," Jerry said,
    "Shows there's good times ahead,
"Though by Babylon now we're detained."

33
"By Chaldeans I drove you away,
"But I'll shrive you and soothe your dismay.
    "Your cities reborn,
    "Dave's throne ye'll adorn.
"My word's solid, as night follows day."

34
You'll lose, Zed, but die in your bed.
Your folks should have done what you said.
    Those who passed through the cow,
    Let them ruminate now!
Should have freed all their servants instead."

35
Sober Rechabites said, "Our dad Jon
"Told us not to drink wine from now on."
    "Hear that, Judah?" cried God.
    "Their pa speaks and they nod!
"But ye stray, so our covenant's gone!"

36
Jerry's prophecies, written and rolled,
Were a hit, and King Jeho was told.
    "That book I'll acquire!"
    Then he set it on fire!
Now his body lies out in the cold.

37
From Egyptians the Chaldeans fled.
Jerry wandered. God told him, "Tell Zed
    "They'll come back again."
    He was imprisoned then:
Said his piece for a piece of Zed's bread.

38
Zed dropped him in mud, drew him out:
"Now mind you say nothing about
    "Our chat, and you'll live."
    Jerry shrugged: "Better give
"Yourself up, or this city they'll rout."

39
Jerusalem fell, and Zed, caught,
Saw his sons killed, then, blinded, saw naught.
    Babylon's men released
    Jeremiah at least.
He who helped him his own rescue wrought.

40

Nebuzaradan caught and freed Jerry,
Who found Ged, who was warned to be wary,
    Amidst all this upheaval,
    Of Ishmael's evil,
But said, "Press your wine! My view's contrary!"

41

Ish and pals killed Ged at dinner;
Killed eighty more, threw them all in a
    Pit and then fled.
    Jo freed captives and said,
"We'll to Egypt!" (But caught not the sinner.)

42

"Don't you dare!" (Jerry channelled) "Stay put!
"Go ye not to the land of King Tut!
    "Let's make nice in Judah.
    "Going to Egypt is ruder!
"Sword, pox, famine if there you set foot!"

43

"You're bluffing!" scoffed Jo and the rest:
"Here in Egypt it's you who's the pest!"
    "Bab's king conquers," cried Jerry,
    "Where these big stones I bury!
"Faithless Jews and false gods he'll molest!"

44

"Wrong gods weren't enough, now wrong lands!
"Ye trust anything but my commands!"
    "Heaven's queen gave us food!"
    "You've much misconstrued,"
Jerry said, "Here you'll die. God's word stands."

45

Through Jerry, God's words to Baruch
When his woes seemed like endless rebuke:
    "What I've built, I'll destroy.
    "You're not titan but toy.
    "Withal, your survival's no fluke."

46

"Egypt floods up and goes down in flames!
"For Babylon wins in God's games!
    "The Pharaoh's time's passed.
    "I'll save Judah at last.
    "Punish, preserve, my twin aims."

47

Philistines, from the north waters rise!
From your kids turn your horse-panicked eyes!
    You're cut off from Tyrus!
    Of hair you're desirous!
God's sword Ashkelon will chastise!

48

Moab's doomed, and soon none shall live there!
Chemosh caught - swap your pride for despair!
    Heshbon and Sihon
    Burn Holon and Dibon,
From the fear to the pit to the snare!

49

"King and princes of Ammonites, scram!
"Edom I'll lay waste and damn!
    "Damascus shall burn!
    "In Hazor dragons turn!
"To the four winds I'll scatter Elam!"

50

From the north rises Babylon's doom!
All her makings shall nations consume,
    Leaving land where none dwell!
    Soon be home, Israel!
No mercy! They've made our God fume!

51

"Babylon's at the drunk, windy stage!
"She'll be ravaged for raising my rage!
    "Israel's the axe
    "To press my attacks!"
Let Euphrates now swallow this page.

52

Fled ahead, Zed who led's dead instead.
Neb's took all the gold goods, quite a spread!
    Fourscore they misuse;
    Enslaved four thousand Jews,
But Jeho they let out and fed bread.

LAMENTATIONS

1
Zion's emptied, its fortunes are dire!
Bowels troubled, my bones are on fire!
    Young men caught, none escapes,
    Virgins trodden like grapes!
Same fate for my foes, my desire!

2
The Lord is our enemy now.
The elders cast dust on their brow.
    Our tears are a river.
    I've poured out my liver.
We're thrown down, per God's earlier vow.

3
For the sins of youth God recompensed me.
To punish transgressions commenced he,
    With wormwood and gall,
    But there's mercy for all.
To my foes, I hope God is against thee!

4
Cruel as ostriches, penance we earn:
By God famished! He made Zion burn!
    Bone dry, suckling's tongue!
    Clad in scarlet, hug dung!
Gloating Edom, 'twill soon be your turn!

5
We're orphans, reproached, buying wood,
Begging bread from who stole maidenhood.
    For our dads' sins we're proxies.
    In Zion walk foxes.
Return, Lord, your wroth we've withstood!

EZEKIEL

1
From a firestorm I saw, way back when,
Four four-faced and four-wingèd men
    Whose spirits were wheels,
    Whose wingbeat reveals
God's voice enthroned. Glory spoke then:

2
"STAND! AND TO ISRAEL PREACH!
"THEY'RE REBELLIOUS, BUT MUST HEAR YOUR SPEECH.
    "THOUGH GLOOMY TOWN CRIERS
    "MEET SCORPIONS AND BRIERS,
"FROM THIS VOLUME LEARN ALL THAT I TEACH."

3
I ate the sweet roll and God said,
"'GAINST THE PEOPLE'S HARD HEARTS, YOUR HARD HEAD!"
    To Chebar I flew!
    "TELL THE WICKED THEY'RE THROUGH.
"IF YOU DON'T, I'LL BLAME YOU WHEN THEY'RE DEAD!"

4
"DRAW ZION BESIEGED AND LIE STILL,
"TILL THE DAYS OF THEIR SINS YOU FULFIL!
    "YOUR FIFTEEN MONTHS AMONG
    "BARLEY BREAD BAKED WITH DUNG
"DEPICTS HOW THEY'LL ALL STARVE ON MY HILL!"

5
"CUT YOUR HAIR AND DIVIDE IT IN THREE.
"BURN A THIRD - THAT'S THE FAMINE, YOU SEE.
    "CHOP A THIRD - DEATH BY SWORD;
    "BLOW THE REST - SCATTERED HORDE.
"THAT'LL TEACH 'EM TO LISTEN TO ME."

6

"Tell the mountains I'll make a bloodbath
"Of all those who strayed from my path.
    "My just genocide'll
    "Spread slain 'neath each idol
"And leave cities as wild as Diblath."

7

"This morning Israel meets its end!
"On its misdeeds its fate will depend.
    "Either starve in the city
    "Or be run through. No pity
"From thy furious Lord shall extend!"

8

Amber-flamed, the Lord's hand grabs my hair,
Lifts me north to see Jealousy there.
    "For this, and because
    "Women weep for Tammuz,
"And men bow to the sun, I won't spare!"

9

"Mark the good guys!" God ordered a writer.
"Kill the rest!" he instructed each fighter.
    "Have mercy!" I cried,
    But God said, "They'll have died
"For a populace smaller but righter!"

10

Above cherubs, God's throne in the sky!
"Grab coals, writer! Scatter nearby!"
    For each angel, a wheel:
    God's automobile!
Cheb's cherub Chitty-Bang-Bang can fly!

11

Men of mischief, two dozen I'm shown.
"Say, this town ain't their cauldron! They're thrown
    "To the sword or strange lands!
    "Those left, keep my commands!"
So I'm back now, our fate to bemoan.

12

"Carry stuff through a hole in the night
"To signify Israel's flight.
    "Allegorical mime
    "Will impress every time!
"Tell 'em prophecies soon will prove right."

13

"Against prophets of lies, prophesy!
"Desert foxes! Who sent 'em? Not I!
    "Their unmortared wall
    "Will collapse on 'em all!
"Armpit pillows will not make you fly!"

14

"Idolaters pay for their treason!
"I'll lay waste the land in sin's season!
    "Job, Noah and Dan
    "Couldn't alter my plan!
"But the remnant redeemed are my reason."

15

"Take the vine, but you will not get wood.
"Unburned, it's already no good.
    "Israel is the same.
    "I'll put her to the flame.
"For their trespass, all Canaan is mud."

16

"Jerusalem, babe that I nursed!
"Of all sinners you turned out the worst!
    "You oblige everyone!
    "And the whore pays the john!
"Don't protest if you're grievously cursed!"

17

"Suppose Israel is a tree,
"And this eagle is Babylon, see?
    "Then if this one is Pharaoh,
    "And those twigs over there - oh
"Forget it! You've ALL cheated me!"

18

"Who breaches the contract is done!
"But the father shan't die for the son.
    "The righteous shall live,
    "The rest I'll forgive
"If only their sinning they'll shun!"

19

"You've a catty Ma, princes of Zion!
"In Egypt's her firstborn snared lion!
    "And Babylon's pit
    "Has the next one in it!"
"Ma's a withered vine, something to cry on!"

EZEKIEL

20
"Sod off, elders! You come to enquire,
"But it's false gods you always admire!
    "You've done that once too often!
    "But still I might soften.
"Meanwhile, set that forest on fire!"

21
"My sword's drawn! They should write their obit!
"I will slaughter great men till I quit!
    "And Babylon's king
    "Will cast the I Ching!
"Ammonites? Ah, forget about it!"

22
"Idolatrous city of blood!
"I'll scatter ye far from your 'hood!
    "I shall melt thee as dross!
    "From your prophets comes loss,
"For they're ravening wolves! There's none good!"

23
"I've two daughters, Ahols A and B.
"(A's Samaria, t'other is thee.)
    "Soldiers blue and vermilion,
    "And even civilians
"They've bonked! Have 'em stoned, my decree!"

24
"Boil bones, for I'll burn this town's scum!
"Now your wife dies, but don't show you're glum!
    "Have 'em swallow their pain
    "When my seat I profane
"And their kids to the sword soon succumb!"

25
"Die, Ammonites gloating, 'Aha!'
"Moab, Edom, you too, *une, deux, trois!*
    "I'll make Philistines sore
    "With rebukes! That makes four
"Wrongs avenged!" (Like that *Count* in Dumas.)

26
"Of Jerusalem ye were desirous!
"Our spoils you sought to acquire! Us
    "On this side will waste you,
    "And when we've effaced you
"'Neath the waves, none will e'er mention Tyrus!"

27
"Tell Tyrus to start reminiscing,
"For soon the good times they'll be missing.
    "The trade in fine wares,
    "Ships, soldiers and fairs,
"All shall sink! Take its name for a hissing!"

28
"Too-wise Tyrus, my mantle you don,
"But your riches won't help from now on!
    "I'll burn you to ash!
    "Zidon too I'll smash.
"My folks prosper when you lot are gone."

29
"Dragon-pharaoh, the river's not yours!
"Egypt spends, since Israel it ignores,
    "Forty years a slave!
    "Neb gave Tyrus a shave;
"He'll have Egypt, to pay for his wars."

30
"Ethiopia, hear my alarms!
"For Egypt, all manner of harms!
    "No, Sin, Pibeseth,
    "Suffer darkness and death!
"As for Pharaoh, I'll break both his arms!"

31
"The Assyrian cedar's our text.
"O'er all nations his great branches flexed.
    "But I cut him down!
    "(Didn't quite let him drown.)
"Listen up, Pharaoh, you're next!"

32
"Beasts are fed on your spread flesh at night!
"Egypt's cities and rivers I'll smite!
    "Sword-slain and chastised
    "With the uncircumcised,
"You'll go down in the pit, out of sight!"

33

"He dies who runs not from my sword;
"Speak, Zeke, though you might be ignored,
   "So the wicked might turn.
   "Let Jerusalem learn
"You're a prophet and I am the Lord."

34

"These shepherds* of greed are in deep!
"For neglect, as they sowed, so they'll reap!
   "The flock I'll bring in.
   "A new peace shall begin!
"*(In case it's not clear, you're the sheep.)"

35

"Go to Seir, prophet! There put across
"My anger at Israel's loss,
   "For Seir shed their blood,
   "But I'll pay 'em back good!
"When they're all dead they'll know I'm the boss!"

36

"Listen, land! I will fill you with men!
"You'll be peopled and fruitful, and then
   "Ye who my name profaned
   "Will return, for I've deigned
"To replenish my flock once again."

37

Dry bones breathed alive in death valley!
"So Israel interred still will rally!
   "Thus Judah, Ephraim,
   "Stick together, reclaim
"Your own land for a faithful finale."

38

"Let birds chew five sixth-parts of Gog!
"Their mass grave is a seven-month slog!
   "Magog shall be ashen!
   "Eat fatlings of Bashan,
"My people, live high on the hog!"

40

In a vision, the city of God!
And a brass man with measuring rod.
   He showed me each new bit's
   Dimensions in cubits:
Gates, chambers, steps, arches and quad.

41

He measured the walls, doors and spaces
Of the temple and neighbouring places.
   Side chambers wind round.
   All over are found
Palm trees gazed on by cherubs' twin faces.

42

From there the inspection proceeds
To the utter court chambers, where feeds
   The priest on his portion.
   This house's proportion
Is square, each side five hundred reeds.

43

From the temple God's mighty voice spake:
"On a big four-square altar you'll make.
   "Sacrifices. You may
   "Serve three slaughters a day
"For a week, then your offerings I'll take."

44

"Shut that door! You've all sinned, start afresh.
"I with Levites of Zadok enmesh.
   "Clean clothes are their purgings!
   "They'll marry just virgins!
"They'll own naught, touch no dead, eat burnt flesh."

45

"Save an oblong oblation for God
"With parts for the prince and priest squad.
   "There's no measures fairer
   "Than hin, homer, gerah!
"At each feast livestock die, twenty-odd."

46

"Take flour and an ephah of oil.
"Cook Sunday roast, wrapped in tinfoil.
   "Princes come from the east,
   "Plebs north, for the feast.
"Corner rooms are where priests go to boil."

47

The house leaks! The stream forms a river
Where trees endless fruit shall deliver.
    There'll be fish of each order
    And the water's a border
Marking land whence each tribe takes a sliver.

48

Dan, Ash, Naph, Man, Eph, Reuben, Jude:
There's a portion for each of Jake's brood;
    For Ben, Sim, Iz, Zeb, Gad,
    For the Levites, and add
The prince; with God's city conclude.

DANIEL

1

Bab's king nurtured kids who were smart.
Fair of face, fed on beans, set apart,
    Az, Mish and Han,
    And especially Dan
Were way off the astrologer's chart.

2

"Die, sages who can't guess my dream!"
"Metals precious and base? Your regime!
    "But the iron man falls
    "When God's kingdom calls!"
Dan's ennobled for telling the theme.

3

"All bow to my statue or burn!"
Dan's mates won't stoop. Neb is stern!
    But they walk in the furnace
    With God, and thus earn his
Respect. With a raise, they return.

4

"Neb here! And I dreamed of a tree
"That got chopped. Dan said it was me!
    "Unbelieving, beguiled,
    "I took to the wild!
"Now restored, none's more faithful than me."

5

King Bel drank from God's cups, and a hand
Scribbled words no sage could understand.
    Dan translated: "You're doomed,
    "For you've grossly presumed."
So Bel died, and the Medes took his land.

6

Dan's enemies plotted to pry on
His prayers; found he knelt facing Zion!
    He was thrown in the den,
    But God cooled the cats; then
'Twas his foes and their kin fed the lion!

7

Dreamt four beasts rose from wind and sea's riot!
One with teeth made of iron (tough diet!)
    And ten horns, of which three
    Bowed to earth's last king: he
Divides time, but time's up. I kept quiet.

8

Bighorn goat tramples ragged-horn ram!
It's Greece telling Persia to scram.
    Four kingdoms - one king
    Destroys many a thing,
But is broken. I'm baffled, I am.

9

Oh Lord, we've been bad, but enough!
Let your mercy diminish your huff!
    But 'tis Gabriel speaks!
    "For seventy weeks
"The Messiah, then things will get rough."

10

I mourned, but then: "Cheer up, we heard ya!
"I was held up three weeks as a scourger."
    "We're not worthy!" I cried.
    "More to come," said my guide,
"But I'm off to complete *Prince of Persia*."

11

"From Persia, three kings, then a fourth.
"There's kings of the south and the north
    "And exchange of a daughter
    "With surely much slaughter.
"No profit in flatteries henceforth."

12

"Mike's trouble. Some dead shall awake."
(All this from the chap on the lake.)
    "They that heed this advice
    "Wait a thousand days [twice?].
"Write it down, for posterity's sake."

HOSEA

1

"Go marry a whore, have a child,
"Called Jezreel, to show how '*I'm riled.*'
    "Then christen your daughter
    "Loruhamah: '*no quarter.*'
"Son Loammi is last: '*you're reviled.*'"

2

"Thy mother's a whore I'll cast out,
"To the wilds, wearing nary a clout!
    "She'll not find her lovers!
    "But my fondness recovers:
"We're betrothed, and my people devout."

3

"As I love, love a woman profane!"
So I hired one with silver and grain.
    "For me you'll abide
    "Like Israel denied.
"Then we'll all seek Jehovah again."

4

"Hear, Israel, God knows your game!
"I reject thee! You'll suffer in shame
    "For your whoredom and wine!
    "(Let's hope Judah is fine.)
"Idols, sour drink and wind for Ephraim!"

5

"His own pride doth Israel impeach.
"They'll seek God with their sheep, but won't reach.
    "For my wrath they're to blame:
    "Like a moth to Ephraim,
"To Jude rot, and like lions to each."

6

God smote! On the third day we rise.
He's our rain! "But your goodness soon dries!
    "You betray and transgress!
    "Gilead? Bloody mess!
"You're defiled, for with whores Ephraim lies!"

7

"Adulterers - ovens that burned!
"Ephraim - silly dove, cake unturned!
    "They're eaten and grey,
    "But they'll not get away!
"By deceit my sword's edge they have earned!"

8

"Blow the horn! Israel's cast me aside!
"Kings unauthorized they've made their guide!
    "With idols they've sinned!
    "They'll reap the wild wind!
"They ignore the one God bona fide!"

9

Ephraim gobbles corn from all floors!
Their sham offerings the Lord God ignores!
    By Egypt be harried,
    Breasts dry, babes miscarried!
Buried homeless in Memphis, the whores!

10

Idols, untruths, you reprise
As hemlocks in furrows arise!
    With false gods a strayer,
    You've sinned since Gibeah!
Wicked ploughmen, reap evil, eat lies!

HOSEA

11

"I drew ye from Egypt with love.
"In no time you gave me the shove!
    "Ephraim, Israel, it is
    "My sword on your cities!
"Tremble ye, like Assyria's dove!"

12

"With wind-fed Ephraim and with Jude,
"Like Jake with the angel, I feud!
    "For no rationale
    "They kill bulls in Gilgal!
"Jake's wife is a sheep!" [This sounds rude?]

13

"Ephraim and its idols - mere fumes!
"Leopard, bear, lion, beast be thy dooms!
    "I'll be king of my folk!
    "Ephraim's waters are broke!
"Dash Samaria's babes, rip her wombs!"

14

"Return and I'll take you all back!
"On corn, olives, vines you will snack!
    "Abandon your fillies!
    "Be as Lebanon's lilies!
"Only fools wouldn't follow my track!"

JOEL

1

Tell your children, and their children next,
How the crop by the cankerworm's vexed,
    How there's nothing to scoff,
    How the offering's off
And even the cows are perplexed.

2

Fires in the dark! Sound alarms!
Ravaged land, God has taken up arms!
    So let's weep, mourn and fast.
    "My anger is passed!
"Now have dreams, wonders, signs and rich farms!"

3

"The Jews were held captive, sold on
"By Egypt, Tyre, Edom, Zidon!
    "Since you were the cause o' that,
    "Ye'll be judged in Jehoshaphat.
"For my folks, a fine denouement!"

AMOS

1

"For three or four times of transgression,
"Broken covenants, violence, oppression,
    "By Tyrus and Edom
    "And more - we don't need 'em!
"I'll send fire on 'em all in succession!"

2

"What's more, Israel, Moab and Jude
"Will all pay for their bad attitude!
    "Ye deny prophets' news,
    "Sell peasants for shoes!
"A big brave man shall flee in the nude!"

3

"With me you left Egypt in flight.
"I roar so you'll hear me all right.
    "Prophesy in Ashdod
    "Of a foe sent by God!
"Summer's houses and winter's I'll smite!"

4

"Bashan's cows in Samaria, hear!
"Sling your hook, with tithes every third year!
    "Clean teeth but no bread!
    "Thirst and mildew instead!
"Since you still won't revere, I'm severe!"

5

"I'll decimate cities! Lament,
"For your starmaker God won't relent!
    "There'll be wailings and woes,
    "For I turn up my nose
"At your meats! To Damascus you're sent!"

6

"Look around, there's no better location!
"Yet on tusk beds ye lie in prostration!
    "Ye cannot plough stone,
    "So I'll burn to the bone
"Ten housemates! I'll raise up a nation!"

7

Grasshoppers eat us, and fire!
God repents! (It came down to the wire...)
    "Shut up!" said the priest.
    I told him, "Deceased
"Are your kids soon! Unclean you'll expire!"

8

"See this basket of fruit? The end's nigh!
"False traders a recompense buy!
    "Dark at noon! Bald of head!
    "Ye'll yearn not for bread
"But my words, while false worshippers die!"

9

"Break the door, I'll let none get away!
"Whether captive or free, thee I'll slay!
    "I'll bring home a few
    "To tabernacles anew
"In gardens of fruit, there to stay."

OBADIAH

1

Eagle Edom, come down from your cleft!
You conspired in Jerusalem's theft!
    Soon comes the day Esau
    Descends on the see-saw!
Of your mountains and lands you're bereft!

JONAH

1

"Go preach against Nineveh, Jonah!"
Jo fled, didn't like that persona.
    But his ship met the blast!
    To the sea he was cast!
Three days in a fish for this loner!

2

Jo bellyached: "Deep in the seas
"I was compassed by floods! Hear my pleas!
    "In weeds I was wrapped,
    "But I know God is apt
"To regurgitate Jo-ambergris!"

3

"Now go tell 'em!" So Jo went, and said,
"Forty days from now this city's dead!"
    But Nineveh's king
    Said, "We'll do anything!"
God relented, let all live instead.

4

"Why do I bother?" sulked Jo.
"'Neath the shade of this gourd I will go."
    It was killed by God's worm.
    "You would have me be firm?
"Ambidexters and cows matter though."

MICAH

1
Where God treads, valleys cleave, mountains melt!
Graven idols he'll gather and smelt!
    So naked I'll howl
    And mourn like an owl!
Prepare for thy fate! Shave thy pelt!

2
Ye do wrong, steal another's estate!
Thy necks shall be under God's fate!
    Needless war thou dost wage!
    The tippler's thy sage!
Gathered, broken and gone out the gate!

3
Ye eaters of flesh, skin and bone!
Ye who offer as God's words your own!
    Ye shall see and say nought,
    For your prophets are bought
At a loss when God ploughs what you've grown!

4
The world flows to God's mountain crest.
We'll beat swords into ploughshares, and rest
    'Neath our figs. **"THOSE OUTCAST**
    "ARE EXALTED AT LAST!
"IRON-HORNED AND BRASS-HOOFED, YE'LL BE
                                   BLESSED!"

5
From Bethlehem comes a great man:
Seven shepherds, eight leaders, the plan.
    Assyria's squashed,
    Many peoples are washed.
On witchcraft and horses a ban!

6
Hear, mountains, the Lord God's dispute:
To him what does Israel impute?
    He doesn't ask much!
    But no more soft touch!
Left hungry, don't drink of your fruit!

7
Still no fruit, good men gone, the rest pointed,
No trust, family ties are disjointed.
    But God is my lamp;
    On our foes he will stamp.
He forgives and performs what's appointed.

NAHUM

1
God's anger is slow, but intense.
His earth-shaking power is immense.
    He'll loose our constriction!
    Vamoose, our affliction!
Feast, Judah, for God's your defence!

2
Oh Jacob, thy wine's down the drain!
Jostling chariots burn down the lane!
    Huzzab's led away!
    All will flee Nineveh,
Where lions and loins are in pain!

3
Equestrian noise in the city!
For Nineveh's whoredom, 'tis pity.
    Like No, she's a no-no,
    So it's slaughter a-go-go!
Crawl away, captains, crown and committee!

HABAKKUK

1

Lord, hearken to me, Habakkuk!
Righteous judgement and law we've forsook!
    "I'll raise Chaldean forces
    "With fearsome swift horses,
"To catch unruly men on their hook!"

2

Though my vision may tarry, 'twill come.
By thick clay the proud drunk's rendered numb.
    Thy shame is disclosed,
    Thy foreskin's exposed!
Before God, the world's idols are dumb.

3

God's from Teman! Say la! Horny skin,
Pest and coals! Sun and moon stop their spin!
    Earth and heathens are cleft!
    There'll be no harvest left!
God's my strength. - To the First Violin.

ZEPHANIAH

1

"Woe betide who for other gods lust!
"Folks in strange clothes I really don't trust!
    "The merchants I'll harm!
    "Wrath, darkness, alarm!
"Flesh is dung and blood pours out like dust!"

2

Be godly, meek! Hide and be blessed!
Desolation is due for the rest!
    Ammon's land will for pride
    Be emptied and dried!
In Nineveh cormorants nest!

3

The wolf judge gnaws on yesterday's bones!
"My anger's on all wicked zones!
    "The proud I'll destroy!
    "The rest sing in joy!
"Ye'll come home, with an end to your moans!"

HAGGAI

1

"You've all houses! Consider your ways!
"How's your deity's dwelling these days?
    "No temple, no plenty!"
    So the folks' cognoscenti
Set to work on the Lord's house of praise.

2

(More harping on Egypt.) "...and then
"This house will be golden again!
    "Ye were starved and unclean,
    "But thy fields will be green!
"Zer and Josh, ye are both my main men!"

ZECHARIAH

1

Don't be like your fathers - obey!
Red steeds to and froing say, "Neigh!
    "The world sitteth still."
    "Ye've restored my goodwill!
"Gentile horns shall four carpenters fray!"

2

An angel with measuring line
Went to survey Jerusalem. "Twine?
    "For walls made of fire?
    "Ho ho! Now retire
"From Babylon, things will be fine!"

3

"Sod off, Satan! Josh, look at this twig!
"Wear these threads, hope the hat's not too big!
    "Thou art judge! Now be shown
    "My seven-eyed stone.
"Meet thy neighbours beneath vine and fig."

4

A candlestick, gold, seven-jointed!
"What's all this, angel, please?" And I pointed.
    "God's eyes, to teach grace
    "So Zer'll finish this place.
"These olive trees, they're the anointed."

5

Divides thieves and blasphemers, this bar
That flies in their homes. Carried far,
    Leaden girl on an ephah,
    Flown by maids on a zephyr,
For a house in the land of Shinar.

6

Four chariots, twin peaks of brass!
Black and white horses to the north pass.
    (Whither red?) South for grey,
    To and fro for the bay.
In the temple let Josh crowns amass.

7

Should one weep at the fasts and the feasts?
God says, "Do it for me, not the priests!
    "Ye won't prophets heed,
    "So I heard not your need:
"Ye were strewn o'er the whole Middle East!"

8

"Zion's life young and old reassert,
"For I'm no longer minded to hurt.
    "They who to my law cleave'll
    "Imagine no evil.
"Ten Gentiles shall pluck each Jew's skirt."

9

"Rich Tyrus I'll burn in the brine!
"No blood for the proud Philistine!
    "The king rides an ass!
    "I play whirlwind and brass!
"Men eat corn, and for ladies there's wine."

10

"It's raining! Bad shepherds, I blame!
"Drunken joy pleases kids in Ephraim!
    "I'll increase thy increase,
    "End Assyria's peace!
"Ye will walk up and down in my name."

11

Lions roar, shepherds howl, forests fry!
You're ill-served by who sell and who buy!
    Break the staves Bands and Beauty:
    We'll abandon our duty.
Potter's coins, lazy shepherd's bad eye!

12

"Trembling cup is this town! Horses start!
"'God's our strength!' say Jude's chiefs in their heart.
    "They'll burn like a heat wave!
    "Ye shall be strong as Dave!
"All shall mourn, with their wives set apart."

13

"Now wash your hands! Be not idol!
"Any parent whose prophet-child's lied'll
    "Thrust 'em through! So keep cattle,
    "For 'gainst shepherds I battle!
"And two thirds will find me homicidal!"

14

Mt Olive splits, shifts to new plots!
Our enemy's flesh, tongue, eye rots!
    All fight that dim day!
    Drought for who stays away!
Jingling horses, and seething in pots!

4

"Soon the proud and the wicked shall burn!
"Their ash 'neath thy feet ye shall churn!
    "Remember old Moses
    "When Elijah forecloses!
"Kids and dads, each to each, hearts shall turn!"

MALACHI

1

"I hate Esau, so Edom's so wild,
"And you priests have thy Lord God reviled.
    "Though ye seek to defraud
    "With thy offerings flawed,
"Let the fame of my name be Gentiled!"

2

"False priests, feast your faces on faeces!
"On your lips Levi's covenant ceases!
    "The strange god ye've wed
    "Is still in thy bed!
"Ye scorn God: 'Where is he who polices?'"

3

"Purest silver my herald shall cook,
"Purging Levi of all kinds of crook!
    "In tithes ye have stinted!
    "Offer good stuff!" God hinted.
"I'll remember your worth in this book!"

NEW TESTAMENT

MATTHEW

1

Fourteen fathers to Dave from old Abe,
Fourteen more dads to Bab, and to babe
    That the Ghost got on Mary,
    But Jo heard, "Don't be wary!"
In his dream, and no longer outgrabe.

2

Stargazers brought gold, frank and myrrh.
Herod slew, hoping Jeez to inter,
    But to Egypt they hurried!
    With the king dead and buried
They found Nazareth, settled down there.

3

Honeyed bugs for John Baptist sufficed.
Wet confessions his river enticed.
    He would Pharisees scold.
    He bobbed Jeez as foretold.
Dove_of_God tweeted, **"Well done @christ!"**

4

Six-week fast! Food, flight, power all tempted.
Onward then, where Esaias pre-empted.
    Jeez from seas seizes fishers,
    And hears pleas from well-wishers:
These from wheeze, sneeze, disease Jeez exempted.

5

Uphill Jeez his disciples addressed:
"The poor, meek and hungry are blessed!
    "Shine a light, keep the law,
    "Live your life without flaw!
"To the nasty be nice, howe'er stressed!"

6

"Do devotions in private, inside.
"Pray the Lord's Prayer, and appetite hide.
    "Forgive trespasses, any!
    "Two masters? Too many!
"Don't sweat small stuff, the Lord will provide."

7

"Do not judge, fix the beam in your eye.
"Cast no pearls before swine. Do not buy
    "From false prophets bad fruit,
    "For sandcastles uproot.
"That's all, folks!" "Well I never!" they cry.

8

Peter's mother-in-law, unseen slave,
A leper and more Jeez can save.
    He let dead bury dead
    And calmed storms from his bed.
Devilled pigs scurried under the wave.

9

"Palsied men I both heal and forgive.
"I fix bleeders and make dead girls live.
    "Blind men see and the dumb
    "Won't to devils succumb.
"We need more men, the harvest to sieve."

10

Twelve disciples Jeez sent forth to preach,
To heal sickness, raise corpses and teach.
    "Persecution and strife!
    "But don't fear for your life.
"I bring families not peace but a breach."

11

John asked, "You da man?" Jeez said, "Jeez!
"Is the Pope Catholic? I mean, please!
    "Still, a big hand for John!
    "But these cities are done.
"Lean on me, folks, I'll give your souls ease."

12

"Even Dave on the sabbath ate dough!
"I'll heal folks, but don't make a show!
    "Don't cast me as a devil!
    "I'm past Solomon's level!
"Who's with, not against me's my bro!"

13

"Ye surfers are seeds sown and sifted.
"Earless corn shan't be borne up and lifted.
    "Angels gather the kernel;
    "The wicked who burn'll
"Wish they'd heeded my stories, not drifted."

MATTHEW

14
Herod's niece danced for John Baptist's head.
Fish sandwiches five thousand fed.
    Jeez walked out to the ship
    Where Pete took a dip;
Fixed Gennesaret's sick with his thread.

15
The Pharisees' charge Jeez provokes.
"On soiled words, not soiled hands, a man chokes!"
    One begged crumbs from God's table,
    But those breadcrumbs were able
To help her and feed four thousand blokes.

16
"Pharisees see the sky's red,
"But naught else, so beware of their bread!"
    Pete won *What's My Line?*
    "You're a brick! Heaven's thine!
"Kingdom comes before you lot are dead!"

17
Jeez glowed on a mountain with Mo.
"Johnny B was Elias, you know!
    "You'd move mountains unflustered
    "If your faith was like mustard!
"Pay the taxman with fishy escrow!"

18
"To gain heaven, become like a child.
"Be rid of a limb you've reviled.
    "Forbear four-ninety times
    "To press trespassers' crimes.
"God forgives: be thou equally mild."

19
"The sole ground for divorce: fornication!
"But don't wed a gal after castration.
    "These children ye'll suffer.
    "Threading camels ain't tougher
"Than for rich men to win their salvation."

20
"When you tend grapes for heaven, a day
"Or an hour earns the same penny pay.
    "Thrones for Zebedee's lads?
    "They're not mine, they're my dad's!"
Two blind men Jeez healed by the way.

21
Ass-borne Jeez cast out each temple trader.
The priests grouched: "Who made you a crusader?"
    "You decide why figs wither
    "And mountains come hither!
"In God's vineyard you priests are invader!"

22
"Wedding killjoys be killed! Get new guests,
"But cast out the unsuitably dressed!
    "Render coin unto Caesar.
    "Let a dead wife's God please 'er.
"Love thy neighbour and God, my requests."

23
"Like Pharisee don't be, nor scribe,
"For they're hypocrites, all of that tribe!
    "Their oaths are profane!
    "They're like tombs dressed in vain!
"For the prophets and wise they proscribe!"

24
"Temples fall, there'll be rumours of wars.
"You'll be killed, on your names hatred pours.
    "Desolation of Dan!
    "False messiahs! No man
"Knows the time, nor what fate shall be yours."

25
"Trim your wick, virgin girls, mind the oil!
"Build on talents to profit from toil.
    "When God sorts sheep and goats,
    "Only he who devotes
"His efforts to good will not boil!"

26
"Ne'er forgotten, that girl with the ointment!
"Eat my flesh, for death's made an appointment.
    "I don't fancy this cup."
    Judas' kiss stitched him up.
When cock crew, Peter knew disappointment.

27
Dangling Judas in death bought a field.
Dainty Pilate to loud crowd appealed.
    Jeez in scarlet was scourged.
    Saints' corpses emerged.
Joseph wrapped him, his tomb stone was sealed.

MATTHEW

28

After sabbath, Mag Mary and Mary
Saw the stone rolled by white angel - scary!
   "Fear not for his fitness!"
   (But priests bribed each witness.)
"Yo, J'm back!" Some disciples were wary.

MARK

1

Girdled John baptised Jeez in the stream.
"Andy, Si, John and Jim, join my team!"
   Exorcisms and healings!
   "Say naught of my dealings!"
But a cured leper blabbed, wrecked the scheme.

2

Jeez forgives and is palsy's reverser.
On the beach he hooked Levi the purser.
   "Why are your chaps corn-fed?"
   "Didn't Dave's eat church bread?
"The sabbath's for man, not vice versa."

3

No withered hand healed points the finger,
But the Pharisees. Jeez picked each stringer,
   Twelve disciples in all.
   "A split kingdom must fall!"
"Your family's outside!" "Let 'em linger!"

4

"You are all as seeds scattered and sown,
"Some withered, some choked and some grown.
   "Though today's tropes are arable,
   "Most won't crack the parable.
"J'm sleeping, wind, leave me alone!"

5

Cast out from one possessed yet unbound:
Unclean spirits - two thousand pigs drowned!
   That man told of who grappled his
   Ills all Decapolis.
Staunch girl staunched, and a daughter's rebound.

6

By Nazareth snubbed, Jeez sent guys
To preach. For a dance Herod sighs
   While John drops his head.
   Five thousand are fed.
Jeez treads water and calms stormy skies.

7

Grumbled Pharisees, "What's with no washing?"
"You keep man's law while God's you are
                    squashing!
   "By ill words we're dishevelled!"
   Distant daughter de-devilled!
Deaf, dumb and all, healed, golly-goshing!

8

Four thousand Filet-O-Fish!
"Leaven leave in the Pharisees' dish!"
   For sight spit sufficed.
   Pete named Jeez the Christ.
"Give your life for my sake, that's my wish."

9

Pete wants huts for Jeez, Mo and Elias.
Maddened boy healed 'cos papa proves pious.
   "J'll return. Mind each kid!"
   "J'll not rivals forbid!
"Severing bad feet shows good bias!"

10

"God made marriage, but man made divorce.
"Eternal life's cashless perforce.
   "Be as children and serve.
   "Thrones J cannot reserve."
New-sighted Blind Bart takes Christ's course.

11

"Near Jerusalem find me a colt!
"Fruitless fig tree shall fail for its fault!
   "A church trader's a thief!
   "Mountains move for belief!"
Jeez declined cue himself to exalt.

12

"Priest tenants deny their Lord's rights!
"Cast the coin to the Caesar it cites!
   "For the angels, no spouse.
   "Christ is not of Dave's house.
"Her gift's more who gives all her two mites."

13

"Temples fall and false Christs shall appear!
"This gospel the whole world must hear.
    "Through you God speaks to kings!
    "Tribulation he brings!
"Keep watch, for the dark day is near!"

14

On Jeez spikenard's poured from alabaster!
"One of you twelve will turn in your master!"
    Poison kisses from Jude!
    Young man fled in the nude!
Peter's cock crew, his private disaster.

15

To Pilate Jeez said almost naught.
Not Barabbas, but Jeez, the mob sought!
    Crucified with two thieves,
    Death at last him relieves.
By Jo to his tomb he is brought.

16

Two Marys find tombstone has rolled!
White-clad youth says, "Jeez rose as foretold!"
    Mary Mag saw him first,
    Then the rest, who dispersed
To preach. Of Jeez heaven took hold.

LUKE

1

Hi, Theo! Gabe told Liz and Zac
Of their son! In six months he was back,
    Telling Mary the same,
    So to their house she came.
Zac cried, "Follow John's peaceful track!"

2

Jo delivered tax, Mary a boy.
Shepherds shared, thanks to angels, their joy.
    It gave Simeon ease,
    Anna too, to see Jeez.
His time with the wise he'd employ.

3

In the wilderness John cried, "Your fee
"For remission's baptism from me
    "And then from God's son!"
    Count the dads: forty-one,
Dave to Jo; Adam adds thirty-three.

4

Jeez declined Satan's wiles forty days.
Local folks scorned his newfangled ways.
    Exorcised mad believers!
    Cured Si's wife's ma's fevers!
To new cities God's word he conveys.

5

Fishy business leaves Si's boat oppressed.
Urged to silence, a leper was blessed.
    "I do big tricks and small:
    "Forgive sins and cure-all!
"New bottles, new wine; but old's best."

6

"Grain and hand on the sabbath shan't wither!
"Need apostles – hey, you twelve, come hither!
    "All you blighted are blessed!
    "Forgive sin unredressed!
"Bear good fruit, dear disciples, don't dither!"

7

"By faith this centurion's driven!
"To prepare you John Baptist has striven.
    "Si pours oil on my head,
    "But that maid who instead
"Rubs ointment on feet is forgiven."

8

"Master, how should seed stories inspire us?"
"All's revealed to the faithful enquirers!"
    The pigs that Jeez launches!
    The maid his hem staunches!
"From death return, daughter of Jairus!"

9

Empowered disciples lack bread.
Five thousand regardless are fed.
    Jeez met Mo and Elias.
    "Be child-like and pious!
"I've no den! Leave the living and dead."

10

Jeez appointed then seventy more
Disciples to go door to door.
    "Though the Levite acts blind,
    "The Samaritan's kind."
Martha serves while sis sits on the floor.

11

"Pray for fish and God won't send a snake!
"My warning's like that Jonah spake.
    "From Abel to Zac,
    "Prophets' blood will pay back!
"What matters ain't platters, you fake!"

12

"All is known! So don't swear by the Ghost!
"Sparrows, ravens and man – man's worth most.
    "In heaven store treasure,
    "For God knows your measure!
"The time comes when you'll pay what you ow'st!"

13

"Repent or you'll perish! At root,
"Dig in dung 'neath the fig, check for fruit!
    "Let bent maiden straighten,
    "For Sabbath beats Satan.
"Many knock at God's door, few will suit."

14

"Whether ox drops or dropsy, mend fault!
"Feast not the friend but the halt!
    "A disciple hates life,
    "Kids, parents and wife.
"You can't season flavourless salt!"

15

"To regain the lost sheep provokes more
"Cries of joy than the other five score,
    "Like the son gone to spend
    "Who returns in the end
"Better loved than his brother before."

16

"The quick steward, when troubles beset,
"Is commended for writing down debt.
    "Lack of faith won't avail!
    "God's law cannot fail!
"When in hell it's too late for regret."

17

"Oft forgive, and serve me as you must."
Of ten lepers healed, nine were not fussed
    To give thanks, but one did.
    "The kingdom's here, hid!
"Some are taken, some left in the dust."

18

"God's avenged on his chosen who grumble!
"The exalted swap round with the humble!
    "Be not rich, but a child!
    "Soon I'm caught and reviled!
"For fine faith this blind fellow won't fumble!"

19

Little Zac in a tree put up Jeez.
"A lord won't reward lousy trustees!
    "I have need of that colt!
    "This rejoicing shan't halt!"
Kicked out traders, ticked off Pharisees.

20

"I don't say who's my boss, but he'll kill
"Husbandmen who abuse his goodwill.
    "For scribes' long robes and prayers,
    "Damnation is theirs.
"God's for life, but give Caesar his fill."

21

"Poor mites count for more than rich gift!
"The days come when folks starve and lands shift!
    "You'll be hurt, and some killed,
    "Before all is fulfilled,
"So be watchful, don't let yourself drift!"

22

Jude is Satan's! Meanwhile, in an upper
Room, Jeez broke bread, his last supper.
    Jude's kiss his fate sealed.
    Ear smitten was healed.
Cried the scribes, "This Christ's own words him scupper!"

23

Pilate shrugged. "Well, folks, I'm at a loss!"
Herod sniggered, while Simon got cross.
    Paradise for one thief,
    Then Jeez died, and in grief
Jo him wrapped and entombed, soon as poss.

24

Three maids found the sepulchre bare!
"He is risen," explained a bright pair.
    His gang were unsure
    But Jeez talked on their tour,
Broke bread and rose into the air!

JOHN

1

Word! It's with God! John B's gig
Is the groundwork for Jeez, Mr Big.
    "I'm no prophet!" cried John.
    Pete and Andy tagged on,
And then Philip. Nat's faith's worth a fig.

2

Mum Mary cried, "Jeez, we need wine!"
Six waterpots poured out the vine!
    Jeez scourged each venal vendor!
    "I'll restore to its splendour
"In three days this wrecked [bodily] shrine!"

3

"What's rebirth mean," asked Nic, "for the old?"
"Reborn Spirit! Windblown! You've been told!
    "Believe, live for ever!"
    "Jeez exceeds my endeavour,"
Said John B. "Through him, God's words unfold."

4

In Samaria Jeez asked a gal
For water; she soon was his pal.
    More Samaritans came:
    "'Tis the Christ!" they proclaim.
"I believe! Make my son live!" "He shall."

5

A lame man kept missing the flow,
Till Jeez gave him his get-up-and-go.
    "Sabbath healing's a sin!"
    "Not if you believe in
"The Son – you don't even trust Mo!"

6

Five thousand fed extraordinarily!
Boat long gone, Jeez walked seas necessarily.
    "Eat my body as bread
    "And you'll never be dead!
"In this dozen a devil's here, verily!"

7

To Galilee! Back then to feast.
There Son of Man argues with priest.
    "On me, quick, slake your thirst!"
    Spite of old Nic, they cursed:
"Ne'er from Galilee prophet increased!"

8

"She must die who did what God forbid!"
"No sinner's a stoner," got rid.
    "There's no hope for you guys!"
    "You're a devil who lies!"
"Sticks and stones–!" Stones it was, so Jeez hid.

9

"Go wash off that dirt and you'll see!"
"Hey, look what the Lord did for me!"
    To the Pharisees' scorn,
    He said, "Blind was I born!"
"'Tis sinners who'll always blind be!"

10

"I'm the good Shepherd calling good sheep.
"I lay down my life, yet life keep."
    "You're not God!" they guffaw.
    "We're all gods, says the law.
"But judge by my deeds! Off I creep!"

11

In Bethany Lazarus died.
Ointment-Mary and sis Martha cried.
    To prove Jeez's powers,
    After ninety-six hours
Laz arose, and Jews planned deicide.

12

Suppertime! Mary wiped Jeez's feet.
On his ass Jeez kicked leaves down the street.
    The Jews were conflicted,
    But 'twas all as predicted.
"Heaven spoke and will judgement complete."

JOHN

13

Suppertime! And Jeez wiped his friends' feet.
"Wash each other's! Don't think you're elite.
   "This bread's sop for a traitor."
   (More of Jude/Satan later.)
"J'll be gone soon, be loving and sweet."

14

"J go now to prepare each a place.
"In mine you've seen my Father's face.
   "With Truth, you'll exceed
   "Each miraculous deed,
"And the Ghost shall my presence replace."

15

"Farmed by Dad, you're the sprigs of my vine,
"And good works are the fruit that's divine.
   "In loving persist,
   "Though the world will resist.
"No excuse for sin after this sign!"

16

"Be warned, you'll be kicked out and sad.
"Meet the Comforter! J go to Dad.
   "Now you see me, now not –
   "A proverbial plot!
"J o'ercome the world, so be glad."

17

"Now, Dad, glorify me as J you.
"Give life endless and power to my crew!
   "You gave me these boys:
   "In them fulfil my joys.
"One for all, all for one, see them through!"

18

Jude's lot take Jeez in the garden.
They fall over, then attitudes harden.
   Peter lied and cock crew.
   Pilate pondered what's true,
But gave robber Barabbas his pardon.

19

Smitten, scourged, purple-robed and thorn-crowned,
Jeez was written on, crossed off, renowned.
   Gabbatha, Golgotha;
   Jeez bequeaths one his motha!
Aloe-myrrhed, he's interred in new ground.

20

The stone's gone! Mary Mag, Pete, one other
Found just cloth that should his carcass smother,
   Then two angels and Jeez!
   Tom subdued his unease.
Sin-remitting was fixed on each brother.

21

Pete, Tom, Nate, sons of Zeb and two more
Found their fish where Jeez said, near the shore.
   At the beach barbecue
   Pete told Jeez, "I love you!"
"And if this guy waits, don't ask what for!"

ACTS OF THE APOSTLES

1

Theo, forty days passed! The Ghost said
To the crew, "What you've seen, now go spread!"
   He rose up in a cloud.
   Jude had burst, so the crowd
Chose Matthias for his job instead.

2

A Pentecost wind gave each tongue
Foreign language to startle the throng.
   Pete cried, "It's a sign
   "That dead Jeez was divine!
"Here's another – sign here and belong!"

3

A lame man gained a beautiful gait
In the Beautiful Gate from John's mate:
   It was Pete, who declared,
   "For Jeez prophets prepared!
"If you don't heed, they've told you your fate!"

4

Sadducees, sad, you see, to hear Pete,
Held and questioned him over his feat.
   "You all crucified Jeez,
   "So we'll speak as we please!"
The apostles shared land, cash and meat.

5

Sapphira and spouse Ananias
Fell down dead when exposed as bad liars.
    The apostles in need
    By an angel were freed.
Said Sadducees, "Cease!" But Pete's pious.

6

"To grease grumbling Greeks, select seven
"Sound servants," said Pete-plus-eleven.
    Thus came wonders from Stephen,
    Whose enemies even
Saw his face like an angel's of heaven.

7

Now Steve whittered on about Mo,
Jacob, Egypt, the temple and Jo.
    The priests at him gnashed!
    With stones he was dashed!
Young Saul minded coats at the show.

8

The church Saul set out to destroy,
While Samaria's sorcerer's ploy
    To purchase power failed.
    A chariot's hailed!
And its eunuch Phil filled with faith's joy.

9

Saul lost sight of his Christian-grab
Near Damascus, where God's voice said, "Blab
    "About Jeez when you see!"
    Though pursued, he won free.
Pete de-palsied Aeneas, raised Tab.

10

"CORNY, GO CALL FOR PETE, BE ADVISED!
"PETE, UNCLEAN IS NO MAN I'VE DEVISED!"
    Pete tells Corny and friends
    What on Jesus depends.
For their spirited talk they're baptised.

11

In Jerusalem Pete told the story
Of how Gentiles partook of Christ's glory.
    Barnabas, faithful gent,
    Was to Antioch sent
And with Saul relieved scant inventory.

12

Herod kills James, locks up Pete,
But an angel leads Pete down the street.
    He plays knock-knock with Rhoda.
    For a regicide coda:
Named a god, Herod dies as worms eat.

13

In Paphos Isle, Barn and Saul/Paul
Blind a mage, save the chief from his thrall.
    So to Antioch, preaching.
    Jews rejected their teaching.
Gentiles lapped it up, saving their soul.

14

Barn and Paul displeased Jews' subcommittees,
But he walks, the lame man who Paul pities!
    Folks said, "Barney is Jove!
    "Paul's that Mercury cove!"
Paul got stoned, but they did some more cities.

15

Circumcision, baptism? Dispute!
"God wants Gentiles," said James, "so it's moot.
    "Let 'em not stray or strangle!"
    With this fix for the wrangle,
Barn's the sea, Paul's the Syrian route.

16

Paul cut Tim and with Silas went on;
Baptised Lyd, told a spirit, "Begone!"
    They were flogged and in stocks;
    Quaking earth broke the locks.
Turnkey's turned by Paul, converting con!

17

Thessalonians persecute Jason,
Paul's host, so to Athens they hasten.
    Graved on Greek altar stone:
    "To a God that's unknown"!
These idolaters Paul sought to chasten.

18

With Aquila in Corinth Paul stayed
(Gentiles, Jews, in the big tent he made)
    Eighteen months, then traversed
    Through Ephesus first.
By Apollos's words Jews were swayed.

19

In tongues baptised Ephesians froth.
Nude exorcists fail 'gainst Paul's cloth.
    Art books burned, but the smiths
    Make a stand for their myths.
'Twas the clerk stopped the turmoil and wrath.

20

As Paul talked, one who dozed lost his grip,
Fell three floors, but no worse for the trip.
    In Ephesus Paul
    Said his farewells, and all
Cried to see him no more. We took ship.

21

With disciples, a long route we take.
Agabus says, "Don't go, for Paul's sake!"
    But Jerusalem calls:
    The decision was Paul's.
Arrested, on stairs, he thus spake:

22

[In Hebrew] "I once persecuted
"The Christians, but I was recruited
    "To talk to non-Jews!"
    But uproar ensues;
Still, he's Roman, so scourging's commuted.

23

"Have him cuffed!" the priest puffed; but Paul
                                     huffed:
"I'm a Pharisee!" Split foes were stuffed.
    Forty Jews vowed to fast
    Till Paul breathed his last,
But by cavalry they were rebuffed.

24

"Noble Felix, this Paul is a pest!"
Grumbled Tertullus. "Give it a rest,"
    Answered Paul, "for no crime
    "Have I done in my time!"
Felix settled for loose house arrest.

25

From Felix to Festus Paul's passed.
By Jews reaccused, he holds fast:
    "They've proved not one thing!"
    So Agrippa the king
Hears him next. Is he Rome-bound at last?

26

"For the Pharisees I was crowd-pleaser,
"Soul at ease, till I sees this Jeez geezer.
    "Now I preach for repentance."
    The King said, "No sentence!
"But these pleas guarantees he sees Caesar."

27

So we sailed to and fro in the Med.
"Rest in Crete," Paul advised; but instead
    We set sail 'gainst the wind.
    All the cargo we binned.
The ship broke: to an island we fled.

28

Paul proved snakeproof, and healed on the isle.
Thence to Rome, for his nominal trial.
    He told Jews his tales
    Of Jeez's travails
For two years, undisturbed all the while.

ROMANS

1

To Rome, re God's son, from me, Paul:
Hope to visit, to preach to you all!
    God reserves his disgust
    For unseemly lust
In men more pleased the more they appal!

2

Do you, knowing the law, think you're smart
To judge others and not your own part?
    For it's not circumcision
    That marks the division
'Twixt good men and bad, but the heart.

3

To us Jews has God's word been revealed,
But that cannot from sin be our shield,
    For no man's without flaw
    And our cleaving to law
Won't suffice: to God's grace we must yield.

4

Now Abe's works to the Lord ain't impressive:
Of his faith circumcision's expressive.
    Not by cut flesh, but rather
    By faith he's our father.
Reborn womb, reborn Jeez, both progressive.

5

In faith justified, troubles bring hope.
For sinners Jeez widened the scope:
    For Adam brought sin
    And thus death to his kin,
But in Jeez do we die away? Nope!

6

Dead to sin, we're fresh risen like Christ:
Our righteous rebirth his death priced.
    Free from law? God forbid!
    No such lusts, we've got rid.
To eternal life now we're each spliced.

7

Wife's bound only while husband's alive;
So sin can't Christ's passing survive,
    For death of flesh purges,
    And all my base urges
I disown: with my mind I will strive.

8

Sin's in flesh, but in spirit we tend
The life righteous, Christ-filled, uncondemned.
    To God's glory we're heirs.
    Spirit works in our prayers.
No strife can the love of God rend.

9

For the Israelites sometimes I'm sad.
By the promise God made to Jake's dad
    We are bound, not by blood,
    And God dooms whom he would:
We need faith, not just law as we had.

10

'Twixt Jews righteous and faith there's a breach.
To believe, one must hear, one must preach.
    In the Lord's name be saved;
    But the Jews misbehaved,
For Israel Esaias can't reach.

11

Are the Jews then cast out? I trust not!
A remnant elect aren't forgot.
    As their fall saves the Gentile,
    A God-graced percentile
May find mercy in God's secret plot.

12

Serve the Lord, for each one has his gift.
Let your love be sincere, business swift.
    Those who persecute, bless!
    Vengeful urges suppress!
Through goodness give evil short shrift.

13

It's God who puts rulers in charge!
Let your tribute their bounty enlarge!
    Five commandments and love:
    Follow all the above
And walk upright, don't drunkenly barge!

14

What should one fasting pick on an eater for?
Shall ye judge? Let your thoughts be complete 'afore!
    To the Lord live and die.
    Let your works edify.
Who eats not faith sins in this meataphor.

15

To the weak and one's neighbours, be good.
Gentiles, glorify God as you should.
    I'll exhort you again
    When I pass through to Spain.
Offer prayers for that day, if you would.

16

Salute all my friends in Christ when
They're in need of your succour. Now then!
    Avoid those who sow quarrels!
    Be wise in your morals!
Everybody says hi! And amen.

1 CORINTHIANS

1

Dear Corinthians, thank God for grace!
By no means let contention displace
    Your faith, bringing schism
    Over types of baptism.
Look to foolishness, things weak and base.

2

I addressed you in fear and in trembling,
Not in wisdom of this world dissembling,
    For mysteries sealed,
    By God's spirit revealed,
Swell our words, and our spirits resembling.

3

Drink your milk! For the carnal, no meat!
Build with care o'er Christ's layer of concrete.
    What you make is his kirk,
    So don't shirk in your work!
Crafty words won't your crafting complete.

4

Faithful stewards, your judgement reserve:
When God comes, he'll know what you deserve.
    Nice apostles, but dim!
    So I'm sending you Tim.
See you soon, and your power I'll observe.

5

In Corinth the practice is rife
To fornicate with one's dad's wife!
    Shun such to the devil
    Lest brought down to their level!
Let God judge, get them out of your life!

6

Go to law over something your bro did?
I'd sooner be wronged or defrauded!
    Settle disputes in-group.
    To harlots don't stoop:
'Gainst your body don't sin, to be bawded!

7

Take a spouse, if you must, but best not.
Sooner lawfully wed than burn hot.
    Though your wife's not in Christ,
    You can still remain spliced.
Let a widow be pleased with her lot.

8

What little we know! But know this:
All gods but God we dismiss.
    If you chew idol's meat,
    You tempt others to eat.
It's a sin against Christ, so resist!

9

The seal of my work's each beginner.
Can't the ox that treads corn eat its dinner?
    Yet I keep myself checked
    And each man I reflect
So in salvation's race he'll be winner.

10

The wilderness sins of Mo's crew
Were devised as examples to you!
    For we're one in Christ's bread,
    Not by temptation led.
Idol sacrifice, chew not, eschew!

11

Maid, man, Christ and God, by degrees.
Unless shorn, women, hide your hair, please!
    But keep yours short, brother!
    Tarry one for another.
Bread's not 'cos you're peckish, it's Jeez!

12

In God joined, still we each have a gift,
As 'twixt eye, hand, foot, ear, there's no rift.
    Parts lofty and nether
    Are honoured together;
By talents we sort, but don't sift.

13

Angel song is the din of barbarity,
Faith a waste, knowledge futile in clarity,
    Without what bears unfailing,
    What is perfect, prevailing,
What exceeds faith and hope, which is charity.

14
Frankly, speaking in tongues ain't much use,
Endless chatter whose meaning's abstruse.
    To forestall a riot
    (Please, madam, be quiet!),
Let prophecies first be profuse.

15
If death is the end, Christ's a dud
And we're mired in sin, flesh and blood.
    Body natural's sown
    So the spirit is grown.
Sin and death fail: the grave is withstood.

16
Macedonia is your precursor,
Then I'll carry the cash - with your purser.
    Salute Timmy, Aquila,
    Apollos, Priscilla.
Love not haters of Jeez, and vice versa.

2 CORINTHIANS

1
From Paul and Tim: Hope you're okay!
From Asia we just got away!
    So thanks for your prayers
    In our scary affairs;
To spare you, I won't come to stay.

2
For I'd make a most sorrowful guest:
Send me love from afar, I'm depressed.
    What I hope as I write is
    You'll forgive all. Where's Titus?
The sweet savour God tastes, of his blessed.

3
You're the letters I send to mankind,
Christ's word in your bodies enshrined,
    For Moses' law heeded
    Is in glory exceeded
By spirit unveiled, no more blind.

4
Not of craft but of truth is our kernel,
Preaching Jeez, and God's heart-light internal,
    So that, howsoe'er troubled,
    In his life we're redoubled,
To see what's not seen and eternal.

5
We've a house that is not made with hands,
Not of flesh, for in heaven it stands.
    There'll be judgement from Christ,
    So let more be enticed:
Through us God's reconciling expands.

6
Pray be better than others have thought us,
Bearing mildly what trials the world brought us.
    Though your bowels be straight ,
    Know but one God is great.
He's in us, we're his sons and his daughters.

7
Let's be cleansed, we've not wronged, great's your glory!
Macedonian troubles - sad story -
    By Titus were lifted
    When he told how you'd shifted
And cleared all your sins' inventory.

8
Macedonia gave when 'twas hard.
Will you likewise your excess discard?
    You'll be repaid in need.
    My boys help you accede
By collecting your proof of regard.

9
Bounty offered, so payment's now seekable;
The amount's individually tweakable.
    Tip up with good grace
    And the saints in their place
Pray you thanks, for God's gift is unspeakable.

10
If my letter's bold, don't be offended,
For 'tis all of us Christ has befriended.
    Let's not unduly boast,
    But we must reach the most.
Whom God commends, he's best commended.

2 CORINTHIANS

11
Your minds I must jealously guard:
False apostles might not find you hard.
    If that seems over-hyped,
    I've been stoned, starved and striped,
Fled Damascus when passage was barred.

12
Knew this guy, said he'd found heaven's entrance;
Heard 'em speak, wouldn't divulge a sentence!
    In my flesh there's a thorn
    That in God's name I scorn.
Shall I find in you brawls or repentance?

13
Third visit! I'll scold if I must!
There's no reprobates present, I trust?
    I would not be uncouth,
    So work hard for the truth.
Live in God's grace and love, as discussed.

GALATIANS

1
Paul and all say: Grace to you, Galatians.
Pay no heed to perverse revelations.
    Keep the gospel I taught,
    For this creed I once fought,
But I'm praised now in many locations.

2
To Jerusalem, where we conferred;
The apostles there liked what they heard.
    But in Antioch, Peter
    Was a too-fussy eater;
Not by works but by faith are we spurred!

3
Is the spirit received from the law?
Abe believed and was promised therefaw.
    His seed in all nations
    Escape law's condemnations.
All as one, you're the heirs God foresaw.

4
Though heir, you're as servant, then son,
Yet you now serve the ones you should shun.
    Abe had two sons, one free,
    One in bondage, and we
Now inherit the pledge Isaac won.

5
Freed in Christ, you can ditch circumcision.
Don't let rogue voices lead to division.
    Works of flesh will pollute:
    Seek instead spirit's fruit.
Walk in harmony, that is our vision.

6
With each other your burdens you share,
For we're nothing alone. Flesh forswear!
    Circumcision don't matter.
    Do good! (Don't I chatter?)
The marks of Lord Jesus I bear.

EPHESIANS

1
Paul to Ephesus: Jesus says hi!
God willed our salvation; that's why
    I name you in prayers:
    "Let them grasp what is theirs!"
We're Christ's church, he's raised up and set high.

2
We have had conversations with lust.
Works won't save: in God's grace you must trust.
    You'd no hope once, uncut;
    Gentile, Jew, now abut.
On Christ founded, our building's robust.

3
I can tell you what none knew before:
That to Gentiles now opens the door.
    I pray on my knees
    That your hearts fill with Jeez!
We know much; glory his, who does more.

4

Be you lowly, united, forbearing,
With Christ's gifts and example unerring,
    Not adrift, but one part
    Of his whole. The blind heart
Of most Gentiles ain't yours - yours is caring.

5

Walk in love, not in filth, and no jesting!
In the dark let your light be arresting.
    Fill with spirit, not wine.
    Wife, to husband align!
For you're parts of one church, not contesting.

6

Children, don't provoke parents to chiding.
Servants, masters - God's not subdividing.
    'Gainst the devilish charmer
    Let God be your armour.
Now let Tychicus give you good tiding.

PHILIPPIANS

1

Paul and Tim, to Phil fellows: Yet tougher
Grows your love of God. Some here speak rougher,
    Some mildly, of Christ.
    With death I have diced,
But I'll see you again. Meanwhile, suffer.

2

Are there bowels in Christ? Give me joy:
Him obey, and soon Tim I'll deploy.
    You'll see Epaphroditus
    Is now feeling right as
Rain, so be glad for the boy.

3

Beware dogs, evil workers, concision!
Though I've law, birth, zeal and circumcision,
    I'll trust faith over flesh,
    Hope that life starts afresh
When my vile frame receives Christ's revision.

4

Help the gals who worked with me, I plead!
Rejoice and in goodness proceed.
    If I suffer or flourish,
    You were kind, me to nourish.
Rich in Christ, God supplies every need.

COLOSSIANS

1

From Paul and bro Tim: You heard preach
Epaphras, and Christ's grace fell on each!
    Offer up thanks and prayers!
    Peace the cross of Christ bears!
God's secret to all men we teach.

2

For there's treasure in him beyond ken.
Don't be drawn by philosophy's pen!
    For your sins were outpriced
    By the circumcised Christ,
So why follow the doctrines of men?

3

Aspire up! Earthly wants are abhorred.
All equal, you're new men restored.
    Loving kindness you've donned;
    With it, charity's bond.
Wives, kids, servants, obey, for the Lord.

4

Be fair, masters! God grant revelation!
Let your wisdom be graced with saltation.
    I'm sending you brothers.
    Say hi to the others!
Spread the word! From my bonds, salutation!

1 THESSALONIANS

1

From Paul, Sil and Tim: We give thanks:
Thessalonians joining our ranks!
> From you spreads the sound
> Of Christ's word all around.

Risen Christ from God's anger us yanks!

2

Though we used no deceitful seduction
You were keen to receive our instruction.
> We're of blameless repute,
> Though the Jews want us mute.

We'd have come, but for Satan's obstruction.

3

Though in Athens I find fortune dives,
Thessalonians' faith, Tim says, thrives!
> Stand fast then, each brother;
> See you love one another.

Hope you're holy when Jesus arrives.

4

Fornication and fraud God won't wear.
Your love with Macedonia share!
> The Lord drops! A trump!
> Sleepers rise from their slump

To the clouds! We'll all meet Jesus there.

5

The Lord's day's like a thief in the night;
Let us watch, for we're children of light.
> Esteem those in charge;
> Your goodness enlarge.

Pray for grace and in all things do right.

2 THESSALONIANS

1

Paul, Sil, Tim again, to Thessalonians:
Glory to you, and encomiums!
> For those deaf to instruction,
> Everlasting destruction!

We hope God finds you faithful, not phoney 'uns.

2

Don't trust rumours of looming fruition:
Christ won't come till the son of perdition
> Is revealed and consumed;
> Those deluded are doomed.

So be comforted, cleave to tradition.

3

That we may be delivered, please pray.
Do our will, work for bread, pay your way.
> Unchurch the unruly,
> But don't unfriend unduly.

May Lord Jesus be with you each day.

1 TIMOTHY

1

Paul to Tim: Heed not yarns, bloodlines tangling,
Which cause doubt, so some swerve unto jangling.
> The law's just for sinners.
> Christ saves new beginners.

Two blasphemers to Satan I'm dangling.

2

Thanks and prayers give, for all men and kings.
Christ's sacrifice salvation brings.
> Silence, maids, and be modest!
> For 'twere disorder oddest

If she who first sinned pulled men's strings!

3

If the office of bishop you crave,
Be sober, once-married and grave.
    To temptation don't weaken;
    The same for a deacon.
If I tarry, know how to behave.

4

Some in latter times will be misled:
Veggies, celibates... Tim, keep your head!
    Old wives' fables ignore;
    Exercise is a bore:
Go and read about doctrine instead.

5

Treat old gals as ma; younger, sister.
Pension those old and good with no mister.
    Let the young 'uns bear kids.
    Dissing priests, law forbids.
Do this, don't do that... [Paul's a lister.]

6

Let servants ensure their compliance.
Withdraw from nitpickers' defiance.
    Food and clothing's enough.
    Tell the rich to share stuff.
Do not heed oppositions of 'science'.

2 TIMOTHY

1

Paul to Tim: For your faith I thank Gawd!
Your folks Lois and Eunice I laud.
    Afflicted, we both!
    Asians turned from their troth!
Onesiphorus helped me abroad.

2

Be strong, work for Christ and endure.
His rebirth will elect's lives ensure.
    Vaunt nothing of vanity,
    Nor prize not profanity.
Be meek, devilled souls to secure.

3

In the end times they'll boast, curse, betray,
Catch and lead silly women away;
    But their fortunes won't last.
    We've God's help when harassed.
Learn wisdom the scriptural way.

4

By Christ, preach! Itchy ears hear the call
Of false teachers. The end comes for Paul!
    I'm left with just Luke.
    Bring my cloak and that book.
Come for Christmas! Here's greetings from all!

TITUS

1

Paul to Titus: Find elders of Crete
Who are blameless, one-wifed and discreet.
    From these, bishops choose
    To help gainsay those Jews
Whose profession of faith is deceit.

2

Teach old women and men to be wise,
Sober, temperate, grave; and chastise
    With sound speech each opponent
    As salvation's proponent.
Exhort well, be what none can despise.

3

Urge obedience, be meek and gentle.
We've been foolish, let's not be judgemental.
    But dwell not on details!
    Shun who heresy retails!
Winter comes! Make your works instrumental!

PHILEMON

1

Paul and Tim unto Phil: Peace and grace!
Changed Onesimus take, and embrace:
>Is he not your own flesh?
>Now my bowels refresh!

Please to pray, and prepare me a place.

HEBREWS

1

In these times God through Jesus declares,
For they both sit on heaven's best chairs!
>The angels are fire,
>But Jesus is higher.

Angels merely serve salvation's heirs.

2

Deaf to Christ, how might we be exempted
When belief is by wonders pre-empted?
>Some guy said, "What is man?"
>Jeez is more human than

All the angels: he's died and been tempted.

3

Think of Christ, our Apostle-in-Chief:
We're house-bricks in walls built to his brief.
>Do not harden your hearts,
>For deceit sin imparts.

Those with Mo perished for unbelief.

4

Unlike them, don't God's promise debase.
"THERE'LL BE REST!" God announced in some place.
>So let's work for that rest:
>God sees what's in our breast.

Jeez knows we're weak, still we find grace.

5

With men's weakness the priest is replete.
Christ's one too, called of God as elite
>To Melchisedec's crew,
>Bringing salvation through.

You are milksops, too young for strong meat!

6

To lecture the lapsed won't avail,
So we'll move on and trust you don't fail.
>In his own name God swore
>When he promised us more.

Our hope goes with Christ, past the veil.

7

Blessing Abe, taking tithe, Mel's begun
The long priesthood, with Jeez the last one:
>For law can't make perfection;
>Endless life's the correction.

Law made priests, but an oath made the Son.

8

Do we have a high priest then? In spades!
He who old terms for better ones trades.
>**"THE OLD CONTRACT THEY BROKE!**
>**"BUT I'LL LIGHTEN THE YOKE."**

Knowing God, the old covenant fades.

10

Blood of Christ does what blood of beasts won't,
As is proved in the Holy Ghost's haunt.
>With remission of sins
>Now the new way begins.

To sin more would be heinous. So don't.

11

By faith Enoch stepped over death's edge;
By faith Abe's family tree is a wedge.
>By faith Mo crossed the sea.
>Woes for each devotee!

Yet though these had faith, they'd no pledge.

12

Turn from sin then and set your sights higher.
Not bastards but sons face God's ire,
    So be wiser when chastened.
    To God's city we're hastened.
God shakes out the dross from his fire.

13

Honour strangers and marriage. None eats
At the altar, and Jeez left the streets
    To die out of camp
    As a holy revamp.
P.S. Tim's free and Italy greets.

JAMES

1

From Jim to the tribes: Faith's kept keen
By its trials. Double-minded men lean.
    God gives good, not temptation;
    Swap your lust for salvation.
Visit bastards and widows, keep clean.

2

Dismiss wealth, treat all equal instead.
Give the starved not warm words but warm bread!
    Break one law, break all!
    Abe proved in God's thrall
With his axe: without works faith is dead.

3

Ship and horse turn at human caprice,
But wild tongues evil fires release!
    For the mouth that should bless
    Will with curses transgress.
Fruit of righteousness burgeons from peace.

4

Great wars from your own lusts begin.
Favour God, make the devil give in.
    Be humble, thence lifted.
    Don't question law gifted.
To know good but not do it is sin.

5

All you gained from your wealth now deserts!
Happy prophets endured all their hurts!
    Look at Job and Elias!
    In sickness be pious.
A lapsed soul's saved by he who converts.

1 PETER

1

From Pete to folks hither and thither:
No longer with former lusts dither.
    Incorruptible seed
    Bears salvation indeed.
Flesh is grass, but the Lord's word won't wither.

2

You're the stones with which God builds his walls,
The peculiar people he calls!
    Those you belong to,
    Honour e'en when they wrong you.
So did Christ, who's the shepherd of souls.

3

For Sara, wives, meekness sufficed,
Unadorned. Husbands, honour your spliced.
    Be guileless and kind.
    If you suffer, don't mind.
As the deluge baptised, so does Christ.

4

Be like Christ, not like Gentile beginners
With their idols, lust, wine and big dinners.
    If you suffer for Jeez,
    'Twill God's judgement appease.
If the righteous scrape by, what of sinners?

5

Feed the flock, elders, don't be remiss:
You'll be crowned! Youth, don't take it amiss.
    Be sober and humble.
    Let the devil's guts rumble!
Peace from Marcus and me. Kiss kiss kiss!

2 PETER

1

From Si Pete to the faithful: Our choice
Is pursuit of all virtue. Rejoice,
    For the promise is ours.
    We're assured of Christ's powers
By God's and, through prophets, Ghost's voice.

2

Mind false prophets, their words are a trick!
But God knows how to damn, who to pick.
    Yet the turncoats unjust
    Swell corruption and lust.
They're like dogs that return to their sick.

3

Be mindful! They scoff who've ignored
The drowned world that our kind God restored,
    But one day 'twill be charred!
    Paul's letters are hard!
You're forewarned, don't be led from the Lord.

1 JOHN

1

What we've handled and seen we desire
To convey, so your joy is entire.
    God is truth and light. We
    Cleansed by Jesus shall be.
Deny sin and we make him a liar.

2

Walk in the commandments, Christ's light.
Love your bros! To all age groups I write.
    Worldly lust is dysfunction!
    You've the Holy One's unction!
From Jeez come all things that are right.

3

Abiding in Christ, sins undone,
We're of God, not of that wicked one
    Who made Cain kill his brother;
    No, we love one another:
God commands our belief in his son.

4

Antichrist spirits deny
Jeez is come. Worldly folks won't hear why.
    God loved us, so should we.
    He's in those who agree.
Love God, love man too, else you lie.

5

No doubt of eternal life when
Greater's God's witness than that of men:
    Ghost, Dad, Word as one stood;
    Spirit, water and blood.
We're of God, kids. No idols! Amen.

2 JOHN

1

To the lady and kids, from old John:
Those kids do you proud! Carry on
    With commandments and love.
    Some doubt Christ's from above!
The nieces say hi! More anon.

3 JOHN

1
Old John to Gaius: You pace
In the truth, and with charity brace
    The church. I forewarn
    Of Diotrephes' scorn!
No more scribbling, we'll meet face to face.

JUDE

1
Jude to all: I exhort you, steer clear
Of those godless defilers who sneer:
    Like damned angels, or Cain,
    They are clouds without rain!
Save some in compassion, some fear.

REVELATION

1
Seven churches, from Patmos, it's John!
At the trumpet I turned to God's Son:
    Paps girdled with gold,
    Seven stars in his hold.
"I'm alive! So write down what's foregone."

2
"Angel Eph: you found liars, lost love.
"Smyrna: devil below, crowned above.
    "Perg: your word is Balaam's.
    "Thya: Jez gives me qualms.
"Overcome nations, win sway thereof."

3
"Since I sneak, watch out, angel of Sardis!
"Come in, Phil, know how warm my regard is!
    "Ye lukewarm Laodiceans
    "May be rich, but poor Chris'ians!
"You'll all sit, for my throne's like a Tardis!"

4
Trumpet called! I saw one throned in heaven
Like a sardine, in front of lamps seven.
    Six-winged garrulous beasts
    Compelled two dozen priests
To doff crowns, cry, "Creation ye leaven!"

5
Seven seals on the book none can read!
Seven-eyed lion-lamb takes the screed.
    Twenty-eight beasts and kings,
    Angel millions, all things
Bless the slain lamb who from death is freed.

6
First seal calls archer white-horsed and crowned;
Red steed next, his sword makes killing ground;
    Then a balance on black;
    Pale-horsed Death at the back;
Fifth for martyrs; sixth, earthquakes all round.

7
Four angels had wind. From each clan
Twelve thousand were marked [except Dan].
    Crowds, each in white robe,
    And from all o'er the globe
Bowed to God, for Lamb's blood washed each man.

8
Seventh seal, and a half-hour of peace!
Trumpets now: with the first, blood's release;
    Second horn drops a mountain;
    Wormwood's third, in the fountain;
Fourth blows darkness. Three more? Woes
                                       increase!

9
Fifth horn sounds, a star falls; from the pit
For five months locusts poison emit
    For the men with no mark.
    Sixth horn, horses embark
Upon killing one-third; rest won't quit.

10

Sunny angel on sea and on land
Roared and opened the book in his hand.
    Thunder I won't repeat.
    The book tastes bittersweet.
Then "Prophesy!" came the command.

11

"Map the temple, but not Gentiles' Court,
"Where for three years two prophets exhort
    "Until killed by a beast,
    "But up rise the deceased."
Seventh horn: God will judge who falls short.

12

Dragon Satan wants sky-lady's child,
But boy rises; she hides in the wild.
    Satan's fight ends in fall;
    His flood pours down a hole.
'Gainst the rest of her seed he is riled!

13

Horned sea-beast is a predator mix;
It's profane, dragon-sent, its wounds fix.
    Fire rains with next beast,
    The first one's high priest.
All bear trademarks, code six-sixty-six.

14

For gross thousands, new songs with no sex.
Those marked, God to torment subjects.
    Cloudy Son swings a sickle.
    Grapes of God's wrath, pressed, trickle
Ten score miles: blood floods steeds to their necks!

15

On a fiery glass sea sing, "We won!"
Seven angels emerge for some fun.
    Then a beast [which one's vague]
    Gives each angel a plague.
Tabernacle is smoked till they're done.

16

First angel makes sores; second, blood;
Third stains rivers and prays from the flood;
    The fourth scorches with fire;
    Fifth brings night; river-drier
Is sixth; and from seventh, hail's thud.

17

On a beast on the sea, sitting pretty,
Scarlet whore, drunk on blood, more's the pity.
    Over mountains and kings
    The Lamb victory brings,
Shown by heads, horns and harlot (the city).

18

Cried the angels, "Great Babylon's doomed!
"Fornicating with kings, her wine fumed!
    "Merchant sailors bemoan!
    "She will sink like a stone,
"For the slain of the earth she's consumed!"

19

The Lamb marries the woman in white!
Bloody horseman sets out for a fight;
    Lands the beasts in hot water;
    Swings his sharp tongue to slaughter:
Birds will feast on the kings he will smite.

20

Ten centuries chained in a pit
Aren't enough to force Satan to quit.
    'Spite of Gog and Magog
    He's cast in the hot bog.
The dead burn who in God's book ain't writ.

21

New Jerusalem, heaven and earth:
Fifteen hundred miles God's city's girth.
    It's gold, with twelve gates,
    Bright with light Lamb creates;
It's his bride, trod by those deemed of worth.

22

Tree and waters of life nourish when
Curses end and Christ comes back again.
    "I am end and beginning."
    To say more would be sinning.
Come quickly, Lord Jesus! Amen.

Printed in Great Britain
by Amazon

35277121R00061